THE STORY OF SCIENCE

Radical Ideas and Extraordinary Discoveries

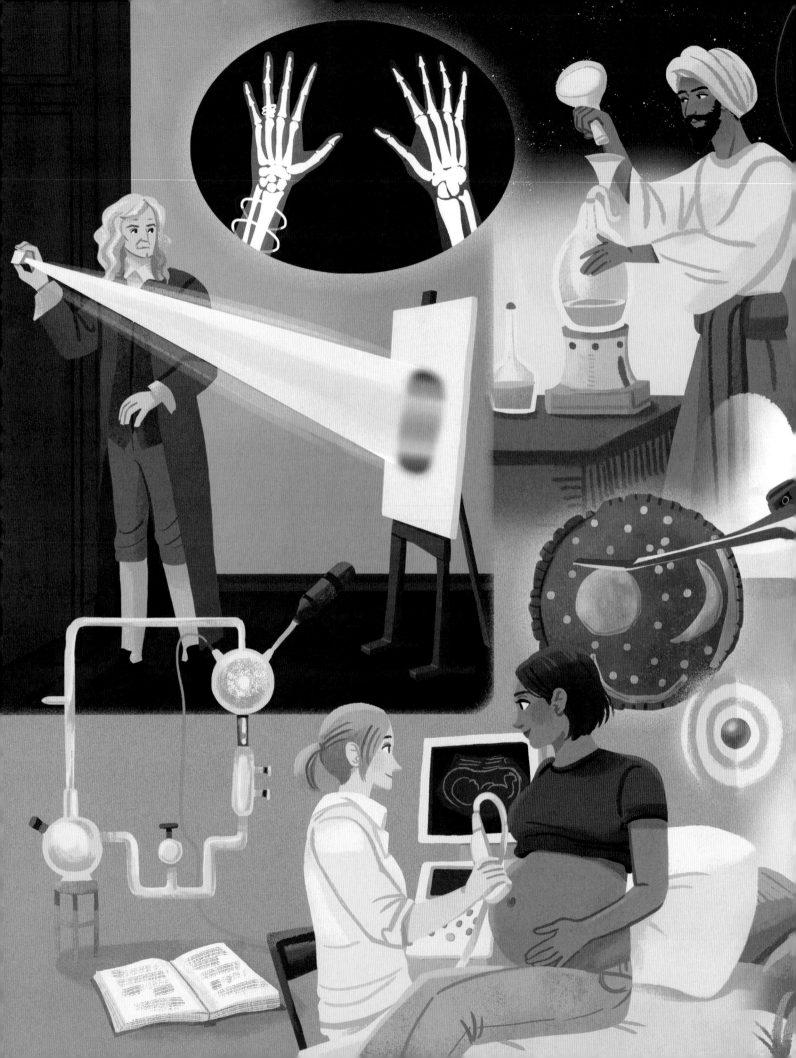

THE STORY OF SCIENCE

Radical Ideas and Extraordinary Discoveries

Written by
Anne Rooney

Illustrated by
Paula Zamudio

ARCTURUS

ARCTURUS

This edition published in 2023 by
Arcturus Publishing Limited
26/27 Bickels Yard, 151–153 Bermondsey
Street, London SW1 3HA

Author: Anne Rooney
Illustrator: Paula Zamudio
Designer: Sally Bond
Editor: Donna Gregory
Design Manager: Jessica Holliland
Editorial Manager: Joe Harris

ISBN: 978-1-3988-3105-6
CH010466US
Supplier 29, Date 0923, PI 00003559

Printed in China

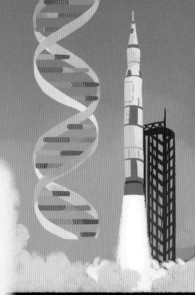

CONTENTS

INTRODUCTION

Humans have always been scientific beings who investigate the world and how it works. From learning how to strike a stone to break off flakes of the right shape, to unpicking the rules that govern the stars and planets, we've always looked for patterns to explain and control the world.

4,500 years ago, people had the skill to carve and move the huge stones of Stonehenge. They even had the astronomical knowledge to line them up with the Sun's movements.

Science stories

We know from old stories, myths, and religions that people have always looked for explanations of mysteries such as how the Earth came to be, or why the Sun seems to move across the sky each day. Their first ideas often depended on supernatural forces or beings. But from the fifth century BCE in Greece, some people began to look for natural explanations. They began to measure and calculate; to search for patterns that predicted and explained what was happening around them.

Making a stone tool requires an understanding of how flint will break when struck at different angles

What is science?

Science is the idea that the Universe and what happens in it are governed by physical laws. This means that there's an explanation for everything, even if we don't know it yet. Instead of invisible, supernatural forces making things happen, events follow a logical sequence of cause and effect. The Sun rises because our part of Earth turns toward it each day, not because a god drags it across the sky. We die because our bodies wear out, get hurt, or get sick, not because a supernatural being cuts the thread of our life.

Becoming scientists

From the seventeenth century, people developed ways of being more rigorously scientific. They designed experiments to test their ideas, and they organized their experiments to discover precise causes and effects. The scientific method which has developed from this approach is still used today. Modern science relies on being able to repeat an experiment and get the same answers. Different experts can look at experiments and their findings to decide whether the methods and results are valid.

Taking their word for it

In the West, the ideas of the ancient Greeks had great authority —and so did the religious traditions of Christianity, Judaism, and Islam. People were slow to challenge these traditional ideas, even when they could see faults in them. But from the sixteenth century, confidence in human reasoning and the development of new instruments and tools eventually allowed old ideas to be questioned and either overturned or corrected. Europe enjoyed a time of intellectual freedom, when people could explore most topics without fear of religious or political organizations punishing or silencing them.

Lazzaro Spallanzani's experiments with birds revealed that digestion is a chemical process

A FAIR TEST

The modern scientific method is based on ideas expressed by Francis Bacon in 1620. A scientist begins with an idea, called a hypothesis, which is a suggested explanation or prediction. Then they design a test (such as an experiment) to see if the hypothesis is correct. An experiment should change only one condition at once, so that any result can be reliably linked to the change made. The experiment must be capable of being reproduced (done again) by someone else to check the result.

Silent science

People have investigated the world in scientific ways for thousands of years, but only some of those people left written records of what they thought. We know from monuments and objects that many early cultures tracked the movements of the Sun, Moon, and planets, but we don't know what they thought about them because they didn't write down their ideas. In other cases, we know a lot more. Chinese astronomers were the best in the world for centuries. They left many records of their observations.

Science around the world

Different cultures have been at the forefront of science at different times. The first were the people of Mesopotamia (now Iraq), Egypt, and the Indus Valley civilizations, and then China. Ancient Greece was the source of many scientific ideas 2,500 years ago, and Islamic Arab countries were the main focus of scientific development 1,000 years ago. From around 500 years ago, western Europe took the lead. Over the last 100 years, science has become truly global, with advances made by scientists in many countries. Lots of scientists today work together on international projects.

Space science looks far beyond Earth and involves people from around the world working together.

The study of biology has gone from whole organisms to considering their physical and then their chemical components—from bodies, to cells, to chromosomes, to the make-up of the DNA molecule.

Cell

Chromosome

DNA

Invisible ideas

The scientific enquiries of our ancestors focused on things that could be seen or touched, from the planets to the human body and the metals and rocks of Earth. With the invention of the microscope and then the telescope around 1600, new realms of the tiny and the vast opened up. Science gradually prised matter apart to consider molecules, atoms, and the rays of energy that surround us. It peered into the bodies of organisms to see microscopic cells and the chemistry that makes life work. A lot of science now deals with the invisible and intangible—how molecules of different chemicals can affect living things, change the climate, or tell us about distant stars.

What happens next?

Science today faces many challenges. These range from practical problems that we want science to solve, to our own attitudes toward science. Debates about science today include figuring out not just what we can do, but what we should do. Should we limit research into areas that could be dangerous? How do we choose which projects to pay for and to promote? How do we deal with people who don't trust science and scientists? How do we encourage more people from different backgrounds to work in science? Answering these questions will help to build the science of the future.

Some people today don't trust science. How can we change that?

SCIENCE IN THE ANCIENT WORLD

Even our earliest ancestors used scientific knowledge. Their understanding of how to use fire and different materials, and what they knew about the lives of animals and plants, put humans on the path to modernity. With their knowledge and their skills at making tools, they could change the world around them. Early humans used science in practical ways. What we know about their science and technology comes from objects and relics they left behind, since they had no writing to record their thoughts or any scientific ideas.

Technology led science for a long time—people discovered what happened if, for example, they struck stones together or mixed molten metals. Then they adjusted what they did to get the results they wanted. They could do this without understanding the science behind their activities. They were just trying things and seeing what happened. But that doesn't mean that they didn't have any scientific ideas—just that we don't know about them if they did.

Cave paintings show that early humans understood how to prepare and use pigments, such as red ochre and charcoal, 35,000 years ago. Their pictures of animals are sometimes so carefully observed that they teach us new information about the animals the artists lived among.

WORKING WITH MATERIALS

The use of tools sets humans apart from other animals. While some other animals use objects as tools and a few even adapt objects to use, humans have gone far beyond this. Only humans have discovered how to control and use fire, too, giving them huge advantages over other animals.

Burning bright

Fire changes materials, often quite drastically. People in prehistoric times used fire to stay warm and scare away wild animals, but also to change materials. They discovered that heating wood and stone in a fire made these materials harder. That gave them better tools and weapons, helping them catch and prepare more food. They found that cooking makes some plants edible that are poisonous when raw. And cooked food is easier to eat— it's easier to chew and digest—so they could eat more. Eating more gave prehistoric people more energy and made them stronger.

A hand axe like this could be used for digging for roots or animals, chopping food or wood, or scraping animal skins clean.

As hard as stone

While some other animals use stones to crack open nuts, seeds, and bones, only humans have shaped stones to make tools for specific purposes. Flint "knapping" involves knocking flakes off the edges of a large lump of flint, a type of stone. To knap effectively and make a tool, people needed to understand how a flint would break. This kind of knowledge about a specific type of stone comes from careful observation and remembering what happens when it is hit in different ways. Making stone tools also requires the ability to imagine a tool—having an idea of something that doesn't yet exist—and then figuring out the steps to make it. Over hundreds of thousands of years, flint tools became much more sophisticated, until extremely fine arrowheads and barbed harpoons became common.

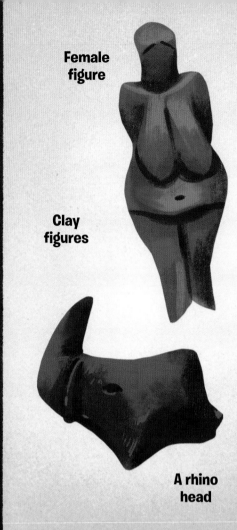

Female figure

Clay figures

A rhino head

People have used fire for at least 750,000 years.

Pretty as a picture

Clay is also changed by fire. Made from naturally occurring mud, clay becomes permanently hard when "fired" at a high temperature. The first clay figures were made in central Europe 30,000 years ago. Clay was used to make pots 20,000 years ago in China. Minerals in clay change its appearance, and early artists used clay pigments, such as iron-bearing clay, to paint on the walls of caves. This was the earliest use of clay. The oldest mine in the world, 43,000 years old, is in Swaziland in Africa. It was dug by people looking for hematite, an iron-bearing rock that was used as a red pigment.

TAMING THE NATURAL WORLD

Our prehistoric ancestors knew a great deal about the animals they relied on for food. They learned when they bred, and how and when they moved around (migrated) to follow food, avoid harsh weather, or return to their breeding grounds. People learned how to use some plants as medicines, discovering their properties and how to prepare and use them. As they began to settle and farm around 12,000 years ago, they also began to change the animals and plants they kept.

Wise hunters

Understanding how animals live and behave made early humans more efficient hunters. They learned that it was best to hunt adult male animals and to kill them outside the breeding season, since that leaves the females to bear young, keeping the supply of animals for the future secure.

A carving of a lion made from mammoth ivory 40,000 years ago shows how animals were carefully observed.

Changing nature

Early humans hunted animals to eat, then used their bones and antlers to make tools and their skins to keep warm. They gathered plants to eat, and they tried to avoid being eaten by other animals. But their relationship with the rest of the natural world changed when people started to domesticate animals, and settled to begin farming.

The first animals to be domesticated were wolves, which evolved into dogs over a few thousand years or even less. At first, humans probably used dogs to drive wild animals toward hunters. Later, they used dogs to guard and control their flocks of tame animals, such as goats and sheep. Animals are domesticated when people choose to breed from those with features they prefer. Over time, this changes the characteristics of the animals. People may have chosen to breed from dogs that could run fast, withstand bad weather, or were large enough to scare away other animals.

Taming the wild

Once people kept animals such as goats, sheep, pigs, camels, and oxen, they bred from those that produced more or better meat, milk, or fur. They didn't need to understand genetics to discover that they could reinforce desirable traits. The same lessons were applied to plants. Early farmers took seeds from the plants that produced the best yield to save and grow the following year's crop. Over time, the nature of the plants changed. We can see this by comparing natural and farmed grasses such as rice, wheat, and corn (maize), and fruit such as bananas.

Flowering date palm

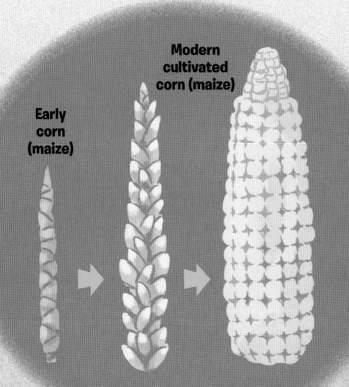

Early corn (maize)

Modern cultivated corn (maize)

Farming fruit

Farmers in the Middle East clearly understood that flowers must be fertilized to produce fruit. They began to pollinate date flowers by hand at least 6,000 years ago. Pollination by wind or insects is haphazard, so people collected pollen from male date palm flowers and brushed it onto female flowers to fertilize them.

Early banana

Modern cultivated banana

AGE OF METALS

At first, people made all their tools from stone, bone, or wood, but later they found that they could use metal. It took considerable scientific knowledge, gained through trial, error, and occasional accidents, to find out how to work with metals. But once humans had achieved this, they could make better tools for farming and building, and better weapons for hunting and war.

People worked together to smelt copper.

First things first

The first metals used were copper, gold, and silver. These can be found as nuggets and are soft enough to be hammered into new shapes when cold. Silver and gold are too soft to make good tools, but copper tools were as good as stone and didn't break. Using copper around 9,000 years ago lifted humankind out of the Stone Age.

METAL FROM THE SKY

Some meteors that fall from space are made of iron. The first iron people used was meteoric iron. It's soft enough to be worked cold. The tomb of the Egyptian pharaoh Tutankhamun contained a 3,000 year old dagger made of meteoric iron with a gold handle.

Tutankhamun's dagger

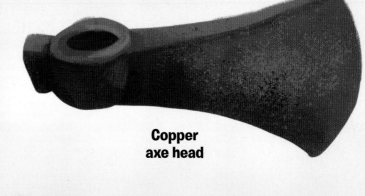

Copper axe head

Hot metal

Perhaps one day someone accidentally left a copper tool or nugget near a fire. It would have softened or melted. This key scientific discovery had a huge impact. Soft metal is easier to work by hammering, and liquid metal can be poured into a form made of clay or sand to produce a very precise shape.

Metal from rocks

While some metals can be found lying around, others are locked inside rocks as "ore." To remove the metal, it's necessary to burn the rocks. The metal then melts and can be separated from the rest of the rock, a process called "smelting." The molten metal can be poured into a hollow form immediately. Metals melt at different temperatures, and people discovered how to extract copper first, which melts at a low temperature, in Serbia 7,000 years ago. They developed basic knowledge of mineralogy, discovering which rocks yield useful metals and how to release the metal.

Celtic dagger

Axe

African hammer

Mix it up

Sometimes tin and copper are found in the same ore, which may have led to the discovery of bronze, an alloy (mix) of copper and tin. Bronze is much harder than copper. The "Bronze Age," when people began to make and use bronze tools widely, began at different times around the world, starting about 5,300 years ago. People learned how to make hotter fires, which meant that they could smelt iron from ore. The Iron Age began around 4,000 years ago. Iron tools made farming easier, and armies equipped with iron weapons often defeated those without them. Then they discovered that adding carbon to molten iron makes steel—a harder and more useful metal.

WATER ALL AROUND

As soon as people began farming, they needed water for their crops. Many settlements grew up beside plentiful water, such as along rivers and in floodplains. People developed calendars by observing the movement of the Sun, Moon, and stars, and used these to predict seasonal flooding. They also began to use engineering to direct the flow of water. This required an understanding of how water flows—the science of fluid dynamics.

A shaduf

People in Mesopotamia (modern-day Iraq) dug irrigation channels—ditches connected to rivers that carried river water far into the fields. They also developed a "shaduf," a device for lifting water in a bucket. To do this, they had to understand levers and how to lift a heavy object by spreading force. A shaduf works like a seesaw. A bucket of water is lifted from the river by using a counterweight on the other end of a beam, balanced on a pivot.

Irrigation channels carry water to crops from a nearby river.

Water above and below ground

People began digging wells in China 6,000–7,000 years ago. This shows they realized that there is water deep underground. Today, we talk about the "water table", which is the point at which the gaps between particles of soil or rock are filled with water. If we dig a hole in the water table, it fills with water, creating a well. Using areas close to rivers or where the water table was very near the surface, Chinese farmers developed paddy fields (flooded fields) to grow rice.

Moving water

Canals are much larger than irrigation channels and could be used to move goods and people around on boats. The first canals were in Mesopotamia, and they had to be dug by hand, often using enslaved workers. When the canal was complete, it would be connected to a river system by breaking through the final wall separating it from a river and flooding it.

Plumbing for the people

Of early civilizations, the Harappan culture of the Indus Valley in India and Pakistan knew most about engineering and fluid dynamics. Five thousand years ago, they had sophisticated water management systems that carried water to their houses and took away waste. As their writing has not been deciphered yet, we don't know exactly how their systems worked. But we know enough about the plumbing to see that it was a triumph of engineering, far beyond anything developed elsewhere in the world at the time. In the city of Mohenjo-Daro, every house had its own soak-pit. This collected waste and allowed only water to flow into the street drain, while the solid sediment stayed in the pit for later removal.

Drains in Mohenjo-Daro had holes for inspection and cleaning.

Hindu Kush

Hindus River

INDUS VALLEY

Mohenjo-Daro

Himalayas

INDIA

LOOKING AT THE STARS

People have been looking at the night sky and tracking the movements of the Sun, Moon, planets, and stars for thousands of years. Even before they could write down their observations, they left records in the form of objects and structures that showed they were keen astronomers.

Sun stones

The points at which the Sun rises above the horizon in the morning and sets in the evening change slightly from day to day over the course of a year. By plotting the locations of sunrise and sunset, people would have discovered that the pattern repeats over about 365 days. People would notice, unless they were very close to the equator, that the days are longer in the summer and shorter in the winter. By tracking the Sun, they could predict the longest and shortest days, when the seasons would change, and when to expect seasonal events such as floods or strong winds.

We know that people did this because they have left monuments that line up with sunrise or sunset at the solstices (longest and shortest days). Stonehenge, in England, was used in this way 4,500 years ago. The stones are arranged so that sunrise and sunset at the summer and winter solstices line up between certain pairs of stones. Other stones line up with the position of the Moon at its most northerly and southerly positions—which happens on a cycle of 18.6 years, showing that people studied it over a long period.

Winter solstice sunset

Heel stone

Summer solstice sunrise

Stonehenge

The Nebra sky disk shows a three-day Moon on the right and a cluster of seven stars now known as the Pleiades toward the top.

Counting the days

Tracking the phases of the Moon is useful for counting the days and months, and calculating when the birth of a baby could be expected. The oldest known lunar (Moon-based) calendar is a 10,000-year-old series of 12 pits in the ground at Warren Field in Scotland. The pits aligned with the moon in mid-winter, allowing people to keep track of passing time. A plate called the Nebra sky disk shows phases of the Moon and groups of stars, including the constellation Pleiades. Made around 3,500 years ago in what is now Germany, the disk might have shown people when to add extra days to keep their solar and lunar calendars in sync, as a lunar year is eleven days shorter than the solar year.

WRITTEN IN THE STARS

People began to observe and draw the stars long ago. Some paintings and carvings more than 30,000 years old seem to show groups of stars. These are much older than surviving calendar monuments.

Planning ahead

People probably used both lunar (Moon-based) and solar (Sun-based) calendars to help them predict regular weather events, choose when to plant seeds, and know when to expect migrating animals and birds. People might also move to find or follow a seasonal food.

Nabta Playa, now in the Sahara desert, was used 7,000 years ago, perhaps to predict monsoon rains.

WRITING IT DOWN

Writing appeared independently in many different cultures. It enabled people to record their ideas, including their scientific discoveries and how they explained the world around them. Through writing, the knowledge acquired by a society could be shared and passed on to people a long way away and even to future generations. Not all cultures developed written language, though. We know most about the science of cultures where writing developed early and people recorded their ideas.

Chasing stars

Five thousand years ago in what is now Iraq, ancient Sumerian astronomers watched as an asteroid streaked across the sky like a bright, fast-moving star. The Sumerians had developed a written language. One of them recorded the asteroid on a clay tablet, using a script called cuneiform. The tablet shows the direction the asteroid came from, and gives enough details about its path across the stars that modern astronomers have learned a great deal about it. The asteroid, now called the Köfels asteroid, struck Earth in 3123 BCE. The Sumerian chart shows that because of the angle at which the comet hit Earth, it didn't leave a crater. The surviving tablet that records the impact is a copy of one made at the time, showing that people were already carefully preserving scientific information.

Sumerian scribe writing with a tablet and stylus.

Sumerian star chart recording asteroid impact.

Written records

Many of the earliest surviving documents record who owned and owed what, but astronomical records also go back a long way. People began to name and list the stars to make star charts in the Middle East and China, thousands of years ago. Chinese astronomers first recorded a solar eclipse in 780 BCE, and the appearance of Halley's comet in 239 BCE.

Secret science

People without written language didn't necessarily know less than people who could write. We just don't have many records of what they knew. We can sometimes work out from objects and buildings that they knew certain things, or can tell from their achievements that they must have had substantial scientific knowledge.

People in North and South America, southern Africa, Russia, Japan, Polynesia, most of Europe, and many other places left no written records as early as those from China, Mesopotamia (Iraq), and Egypt. Polynesian navigators knew in detail about the stars, tides, and the habits and living places of sea creatures and birds, yet left no records. They used their knowledge to move around the Pacific Ocean in the period 3,000 BCE—1,000 BCE, using outrigger canoes. Their journeys would have been long and dangerous, impossible without detailed knowledge of the sea and sky.

Polynesian people used star maps made of sand and shells.

MENDING BODIES

Medical science combines knowledge of the body and pharmacology—how to make and use medicines. It's separate from superstitious ways of treating sick or injured people, such as praying, making offerings to gods, or using charms and spells (though these are sometimes used alongside medical science, even today). It's likely that people realized early that if they held limbs still, broken bones could heal, and if they bound or held the edges of wounds together, new skin would cover the gap. But at least 7,000 years ago, some groups began to use more specific and alarming interventions and treatments.

LESSONS FROM THE DEAD

In mummifying their dead, the ancient Egyptians removed organs and preserved them separately—except the brain, which they threw away. They learned a lot about the insides of human bodies by cutting them open. Many other cultures banned cutting dead bodies.

Coptic jars for preserving organs

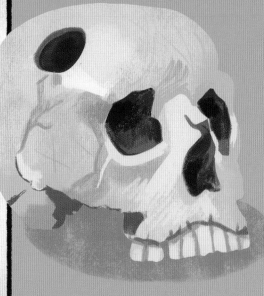

A trephined skull

A hole in the head

The earliest known surgical treatment is called trephining (or trepanning) and consists of cutting, drilling, or scraping a hole in the patient's head, going through the skull. There are many trephined skulls with new bone growth from up to 7,000 years ago, showing that patients survived—and sometimes went back for further operations. The first people who carried out trephining didn't leave written records. The practice was described later in writings from Mesopotamia and Egypt, where doctors applied plants and fresh meat to the wound to reduce bleeding.

Some societies used trephining until recently (and it occasionally still happens!). In modern times it was usually a treatment for headaches, epilepsy, or to reduce pressure after a head injury. It's likely that early practitioners were treating the same problems—and maybe possession by spirits.

Clear-sighted

The Egyptians wrote medical texts on papyrus that mixed spiritual and practical efforts to cure sick or injured people. A document written around 3,000 BCE divides medical conditions into those that can be treated and those that are hopeless cases. The text gives recommendations for treatment where possible. One of the ailments that could be treated early was cataracts, a condition in which the lens of the eye becomes cloudy and the patient can't see well. Early physicians could remove the lens with a fine tool, clearing the person's vision. Their vision would never be quite as good, but it was still better than having cataracts.

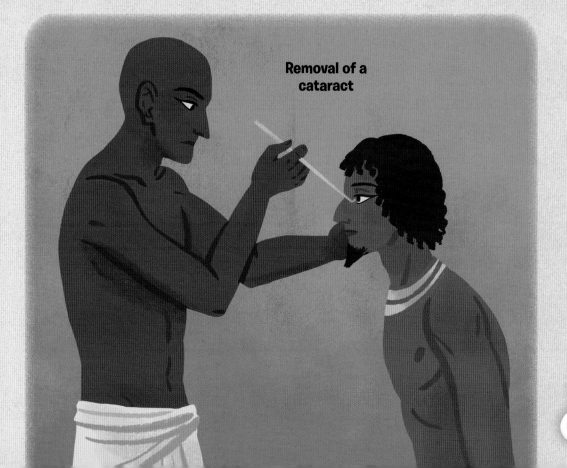

Removal of a cataract

CHEMISTRY ISN'T MAGIC

Chemistry is the science of substances, their properties, and how they react together and change. Chemical knowledge is used to make new substances or to change the properties of materials. Early knowledge of chemistry was used to make pigments, medicines, and perfumes; using yeast to make alcohol or bread; and using a tarry substance called natron to preserve bodies or make ships waterproof.

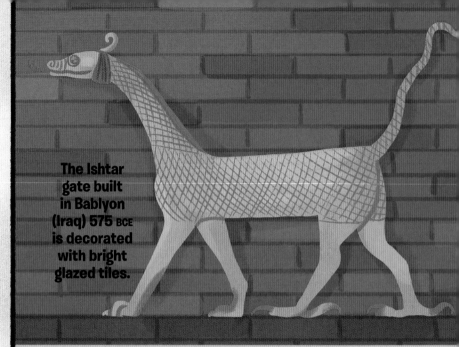

The Ishtar gate built in Bablyon (Iraq) 575 BCE is decorated with bright glazed tiles.

A brighter life

Pigments can be made from minerals or plant material (vegetable dyes). The first pigments were made from clay rich in minerals and were used for painting walls, objects, and probably people's bodies. Ochre is a form of clay containing iron oxide and was used at least 100,000 years ago to make shades of yellow, orange, and red. Charcoal could be used to add black lines, and chalk for white. From 7,000 years ago, charcoal and ochre were also used for tattoos. Later, people made plant-based dyes to dye fabric and paint on their skin, and discovered how to make tinted glass and glazes to decorate objects such as containers, beads, and tiles.

Egyptian faience, a type of pottery.

From clay to glass

Clay is found naturally in the ground. Exposed to the air, it dries out and becomes hard. Firing clay at a high temperature makes strong, useful pots and bowls. Some of the best early pottery was made by the Halaf people in Syria and Mesopotamia from 6500–5500 BCE. They made brightly patterned pottery with glazes from heated minerals.

A glaze is a layer of glass over the surface of clay. Glass is made of silicon oxide, the main component of sand. People probably found out how to glaze pots accidentally, by putting a hot clay pot on sand. The sand would melt and fuse to the surface, making a glaze. Adding minerals can change the hue of the glaze. The oldest known artificial pigment is "Egyptian blue," made using copper salts from 3250 BCE. From around 1500 BCE, people in Egypt began to use glass directly, without a base of clay.

Plant perfumes

Another early use of chemistry was to make perfumes and
scented incense, as the Persians and Egyptians did, often using
oils from plants. But the Cretans went further, around 4,000
years ago, making scented oils at scale in perfume "factories."

Making fermented drinks, such as beer and wine, uses yeast (a fungus) which produces
enzymes that turn the sugar in fruit or grain into alcohol. Perhaps as long as 9,000
years ago people began adding yeasty froth from beer to bread dough. The yeast
worked on flour in the dough, producing bubbles of gas and making the bread rise.

THE START OF SCIENCE

When people first began to record their scientific discoveries, they didn't think of it as "science." The study of the human body aimed to help people who were sick or injured, rather than being interested in how the body works for its own sake. Astronomy was part of a non-scientific view of the world. People studied the heavens to predict eclipses and planetary conjunctions, and to spot unusual events such as the visit of a comet. These were taken as insights into the will of the gods or the unfolding future. People from China to Europe, through India and western Asia, were happy to accept the gods as the only explanation for how and why things happened. But around 600 BCE, that began to change, starting with the Ancient Greeks.

THE FIRST SCIENTISTS

Science offered a new way of interpreting and explaining the world that didn't rely on supernatural beings. It gave humans the chance to take responsibility for their lives, as they came to see that events had natural causes. People also began to ask questions about the natural world that served no purpose except increasing their knowledge and understanding.

Thales of Miletus

A scientific mind

The first person known to have taken a scientific approach to understanding the world was Thales of Miletus, who lived in an area that's now in Turkey. Born around 624 BCE, Thales might not have written down his ideas, but later writers credited him with several discoveries. He's said to have predicted an eclipse in 585 BCE, to have suggested that Earth and everything on it originally came from water, and to have discovered some properties of the geometry of triangles. These ideas point to underlying scientific laws or patterns—that events, shapes, and numbers follow rules we can work out, and that things change in natural ways.

Mind over myth

You can only predict an eclipse if you realize that eclipses happen on a regular cycle, not because of unpredictable gods. If you understand that the Earth started off as magma and changed through natural processes, you don't need a god to separate land and sea, or to create a world separate from a heaven. Thales believed that, with enough knowledge, we can explain the world without resorting to mysteries or supernatural beings.

The measure of Earth

One of the earliest known scientific experiments was carried out by Eratosthenes in Egypt in the third century BCE. He used science and mathematics to calculate the circumference of Earth. He knew that in Syrene, a city to the south, shadows disappeared entirely on June 21 (the longest day of the year in the northern hemisphere) and sunlight fell into a deep well that was usually in shadow. He realized that this meant the Sun was directly overhead. In Alexandria, a city to the north of Syrene, objects always cast a shadow, even on June 21, meaning that the Sun was never directly overhead. This could be explained if the Earth was curved. By measuring the angle of a shadow cast in Alexandria when the Sun was overhead in Syrene, he could work out the circumference of Earth.

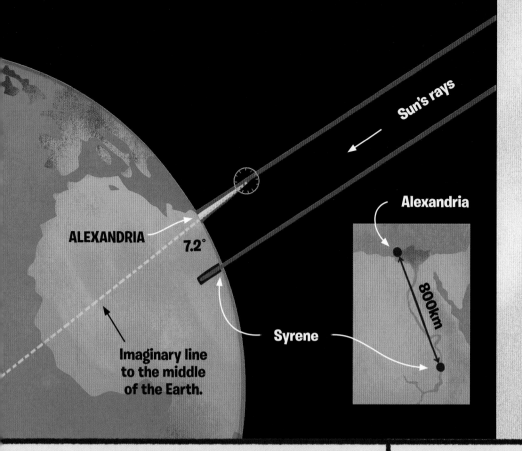

Sun's rays

ALEXANDRIA

7.2°

Imaginary line
to the middle
of the Earth.

Syrene

Alexandria

800km

Eratosthenes observed that the angle between a pillar in Alexandria and its shadow was about one fiftieth of a circle (about 7 degrees). The size of Earth would then be 50 times the distance between Syrene and Alexandria, which he had measured at 5,000 "stadia." (We don't know the exact size of a stadia, but it was probably between 175 m (575 ft) and 210 m (690 ft).) That made the circumference of Earth 250,000 stadia. His calculation was between 10 percent and 30 percent higher than Earth's actual circumference—which is not bad for a first attempt, calculated using only a pillar.

**SYRENE on the
longest day.**

**Sun directly overhead, lighting
up the inside of the well.**

**ALEXANDRIA on
the longest day.**

**Sun casting a shadow
at 7.2 degree angle.**

IN BALANCE

Most early models of health and disease relied on an idea of balance—that when the body and spirit were balanced, a person would be healthy. If there was imbalance in the body or mind, the person would be ill. The idea of the healthy body being in balance emerged in many places and is still current, though we express it differently now. Today, we talk about a "balanced" diet and maintaining the right levels of various chemicals in the body.

THE FOUR ELEMENTS

Fire

Earth

Air

Water

Elements and humors

In Ancient Greece, the body was described in terms of four "humors" that must be in balance. This system was taken from the Greek model of matter being made up of four "elements": fire, air, water, and earth. Each of these had two of the qualities hot, cold, wet, and dry. The corresponding humors were four fluids found in the body: blood, yellow bile, black bile, and phlegm. This model of the body was described by Hippocrates around 400 BCE and remained important to medicine in the western world until the 1800s.

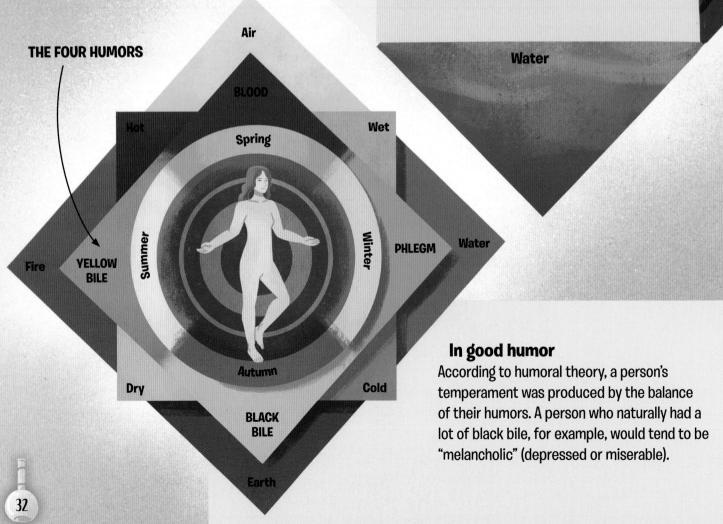

THE FOUR HUMORS

Air

BLOOD

Hot

Wet

Spring

Summer

Winter

Fire

YELLOW BILE

PHLEGM

Water

Autumn

Dry

Cold

BLACK BILE

Earth

In good humor

According to humoral theory, a person's temperament was produced by the balance of their humors. A person who naturally had a lot of black bile, for example, would tend to be "melancholic" (depressed or miserable).

Illness was caused by an imbalance of humors, and rebalancing them restored health. If the doctor decided a patient had too much blood, he would use bloodletting—deliberately cutting the patient, or putting bloodsucking leeches on their body. If they had too much black bile, which was considered cold and dry, hot baths were recommended to provide heat and moisture.

Bloodletting

PEOPLE OF SCIENCE

Hippocrates (460—370 BCE) lived in Greece ,where he founded a medical school. About 60 medical books are linked to him and probably reflect his teachings. These recommend a healthy diet and exercise. They emphasize that disease has natural causes and is not inflicted by the gods, as many people believed back then.

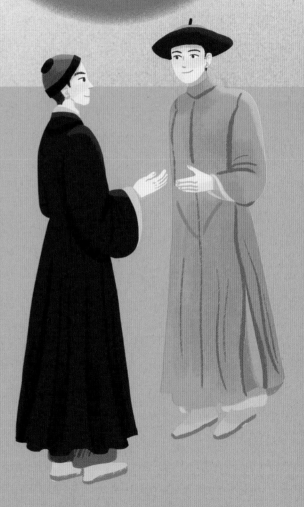

Yang **Yin**

On balance
Chinese doctors had a different idea of balance. They believed that energy ("qi") had to flow through the body, and this was managed by balancing "yin" and "yang." The concept of yin and yang is more than 3,000 years old. It represents two complementary parts that everything can be divided into, such as light and shade, heat and cold, or male and female. In medicine, yin was associated with heat and its results, such as night sweats, a dry mouth and throat, and a racing heart. Yang was linked with cold—the common cold, cold limbs, pale skin, and a slow pulse.

Chinese doctors chose medications to treat symptoms by rebalancing yin and yang. Modern western medicine examines symptoms to work out an underlying cause, then treats that instead.

THE FIRST DOCTORS

Medicine is one of the most obviously useful forms of science. The first doctors investigated how the body works and tried methods of treating illness and injury so that people could enjoy better health. Looking inside bodies—usually dead bodies—revealed what some of the structures inside them do, but it was forbidden in many cultures.

Doctors, demons, and diseases

The Egyptian Ebers papyrus, from about 1500 BCE, includes charms to turn away disease-causing demons ... but also remedies for conditions including burns and growths, and an explanation of how to remove the parasitic guinea worm by winding it around a stick (a method still used today). Conditions described include depression and dementia, showing that Egyptian doctors recognized mental health as part of their work.

Removing a cataract

Early eye surgery

Two early Indian medical texts that are over 2,000 years old show that Indian doctors understood the importance of a good diet, hygiene, and exercise to staying healthy. *Suśruta-sa hitā* (Sushruta's Compendium) gathers together practical treatments for common conditions such as broken bones, dislocated joints, and cataracts. It seems likely also that early Indian doctors used ants as sutures (stitches). They would hold the edges of a wound together and persuade an ant to bite through the skin, then snap its head off. The head remained on the wound, the jaws holding it closed.

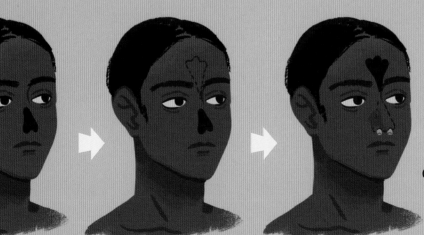

Indian doctors introduced the first plastic surgery, recreating noses that had been cut off in battle or as a punishment. They used a flap of skin, folded down from the forehead, to grow new skin over the wound. Their texts discuss how to diagnose illnesses and injuries, as well as explaining recommended treatments for common problems.

Recreating a nose with plastic surgery

TO THE POINT

Skilled Indian surgeons developed medical tools for use in surgery. Many of these are still used today, including curved needles to stitch wounds, probes, hooks, and knives.

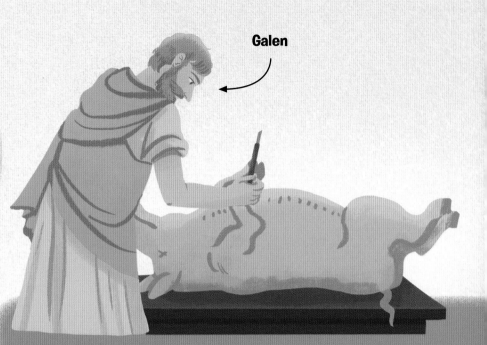

Galen

Medical mistakes

In Europe, treatments were not as advanced. Galen was a surgeon who worked with Roman gladiators in the second century CE. His advice was followed in Europe for 1,500 years, but a lot of it was wrong! Many of his ideas came from dissecting (cutting open) animals, which are not always the same inside as humans. His model of the body and disease was based on Greek humoral theory, and many of his treatments involved bloodletting, making patients vomit, and using hot or cold baths.

Doctors in training learned to make sutures (stitches) by practising on animal stomachs or even large vegetables. They were not allowed to cut up dead bodies to find out about them, but they had a way of working around this rule. They suspended a dead body in a cage in a river and observed it as it rotted away or was eaten by fish.

Practising sutures

MAKING MATTER

Astronomy was useful for keeping track of time. Medicine and anatomy were useful for helping people live healthy lives. Some other areas of science were interesting only for their own sake. As long ago as 500 BCE, the Ancient Greeks wondered whether matter is made of tiny particles or whether it's continuous. This might not sound very important, but it has far-reaching implications.

Achilles

First atoms

Around 480 BCE, the philosopher Parmenides thought that the Universe was filled completely with matter, with no gaps. Around the same time, Leucippus and Democritus suggested the opposite—that matter is made of tiny, indivisible particles. Democritus called these particles "uncuttables" or "atomos," from which we get the word "atom." To modern scientists, an atom is the smallest particle of matter that can be identified as one of the chemical elements.

If matter is divided into tiny particles, it isn't continuous, because there are gaps between the atoms. A gap that contains nothing (not even air) is a void—or a vacuum, in modern terms. For Parmenides and some thinkers, the idea of a void was unacceptable. They thought that it meant that "nothing" becomes something, which doesn't make sense.

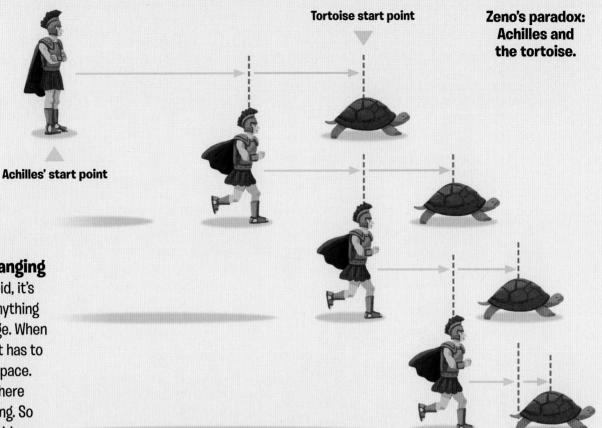

Tortoise start point

Achilles' start point

Moving and changing

But if there's no void, it's hard to see how anything can move or change. When an object moves, it has to go into an empty space. It can't go where there is already something. So there must be a void, or nothing could ever move.

To demonstrate the problem, another Greek thinker called Zeno (490—430 BCE) wrote several pardoxes, which are stories describing situations that are hard to explain. In one famous paradox, he described a race between the hero Achilles and a tortoise. Although Achilles can run very fast and tortoises move slowly, Zeno argued that if the tortoise starts first, Achilles can never catch up. By the time Achilles reaches the tortoise's starting position, the tortoise has moved on. It has moved on again by the time Achilles gets to its second position, and so on. Unless we set a limit to how small a portion of time or distance can be, the tortoise should always stay ahead of Achilles, even if only by a very tiny amount.

Matter in motion

One response to the problem of how things can move if matter is continuous, is to make all movement circular. If something moves in a circle, it replaces only part of itself as it moves forward. The Greek thinker Aristotle suggested that space was filled with a special type of matter which moves in circles around Earth, carrying the stars and planets with it.

BEYOND OUR WORLD

The early astronomers of Mesopotamia, Egypt, and China named and listed stars. They described constellations from the patterns they saw in the night sky, and tracked the movements of the Sun and Moon. They identified the five planets that are visible without a telescope: Mercury, Venus, Mars, Jupiter, and Saturn. But they left no explanations of how they thought the Universe was structured. The Greeks were the first to do that.

Ptolemy used instruments to observe the sky.

Twinkle, twinkle, little star

Today, we know that the planets orbit (go around) the Sun, while the stars are other suns which are very far away. Yet both planets and stars appear as tiny spots of light in the night sky. Chinese astronomers named stars as early as 1300 BCE and recorded unusual events, such as eclipses and comets. Mesopotamian astronomers worked out that the stars and planets were different around 700–800 BCE. Stars twinkle in the night sky, but planets glow steadily. The stars move together around a point above Earth, but each planet moves independently against the background stars. From 1800 BCE, astronomer-priests in Mesopotamia tracked the rising and setting of planets over hundreds of years to make calendars and predictions.

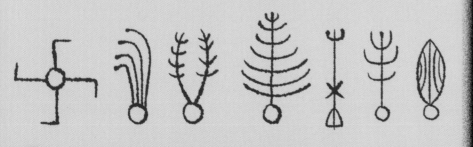

Chinese astronomers drew different types of comets they saw.

Going geocentric

Around 380 BCE, the Turkish–Greek astronomer Eudoxus of Cnidus suggested that the Sun and other planets orbit Earth. He described a complicated system of spheres nested inside each other which explained and predicted the planets' movements. It became widely believed that Earth was in the middle of the Universe. This is called a geocentric system. From Earth, it does look like the planets, Sun, and Moon move across the sky, as if they were orbiting Earth. But their movements would look the same from Earth whether the Sun or Earth was in the middle.

Star speeds

The Greeks ordered the planets, Sun, and Moon according to how long they seemed to take to orbit Earth. The Moon was closest, then Mercury, followed by Venus, and then the Sun. The remaining planets followed. The stars lay in a fixed outer shell, all moving together.

Saturn

Jupiter

Mars

Sun

Venus

Mercury

Moon

Earth

All the stars

Mars seems to loop backward occasionally, but that's just because Earth is also moving.

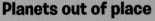

Mars

Sun

Earth

Planets out of place

Because Earth is not really at the middle of the solar system, the geocentric system doesn't quite work. Mars, Jupiter, and Saturn seem to go backward occasionally in their orbits, called retrograde movement.

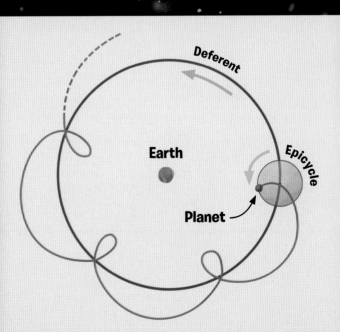

Deferent

Earth

Epicycle

Planet

The Greeks came up with a way of predicting and explaining this movement, later refined by the Egyptian-Roman astronomer Ptolemy. This. He thought that each planet was going around in a small circle, which he called an epicycle, and that epicycle was itself going around Earth in a larger circle he called the "deferent." This would produce the loops in its movement seen from Earth.

NAMING NAMES

Putting things into groups helps us to think and talk about the world around us, but it also affects how we treat things. We have different ideas about how we should treat an animal, a plant, and a stone, for example.

Animal, vegetable, mineral

The whole world can be divided roughly into two categories—living and non-living things. Early scientists divided the living world into plants and animals, and divided these further into groups based on obvious differences and similarities.

The first biologist

The Greek thinker Aristotle (384–322 BCE) was the first person to study living things systematically, starting the subject we now call biology. He grouped living things by their innate (in-built) characteristics. He thought that different classes of "soul" gave living things their abilities. A plant has only a "nutritive" soul—it takes nourishment and can live, grow, and reproduce. An animal has a "sensitive" soul—it has senses and can respond to the world around it. A human has a "rational" soul and can reason, remember, and feel.

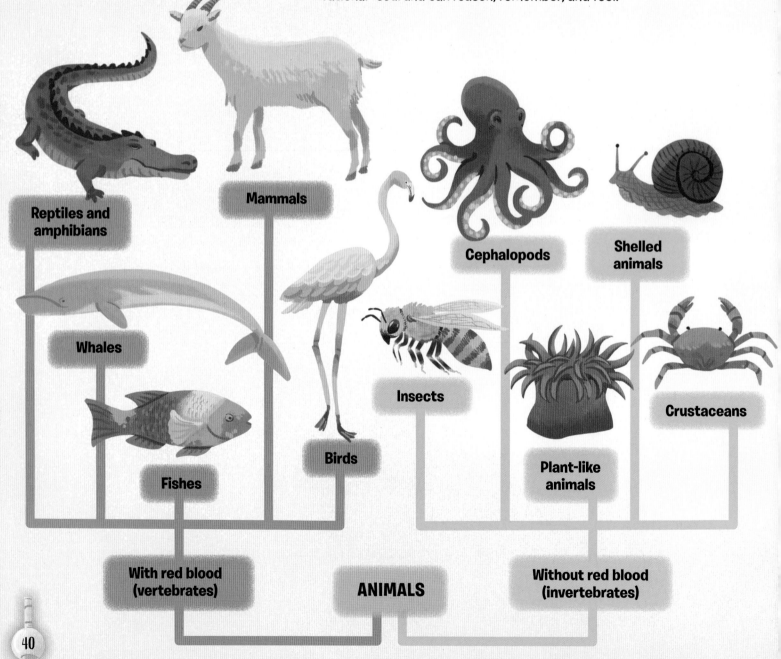

Reptiles and amphibians

Mammals

Cephalopods

Shelled animals

Whales

Insects

Crustaceans

Fishes

Birds

Plant-like animals

With red blood (vertebrates)

ANIMALS

Without red blood (invertebrates)

Animated animals

Aristotle noted that all animals die, and they all breathe, but they have lots of other differences. Animals move in different ways, such as swimming, walking, flying, or slithering. They have different body structures (such as wings, fins, and tails), different ways of life, and different characters. He divided animals that have red blood from those that don't, and then put them into groups, such as birds and fish. From there, it was possible to tease out differences between, say, a crow and an owl. No scientist tried such systematic grouping again for around 2,000 years.

Around the same time, Theophrastus studied plants. He grouped plants by how they reproduce, where they grow, their sizes, and their practical uses to humans. The last of these is not an innate feature of plants, and tells us nothing about the plants themselves.

PEOPLE OF SCIENCE

Aristotle was one of the most important and influential Greek thinkers. While others came up with theories about the world by simply thinking logically about it, Aristotle suggested a scientific approach. He valued observation, investigation, and testing everything we're told to see if it matches the evidence around us.

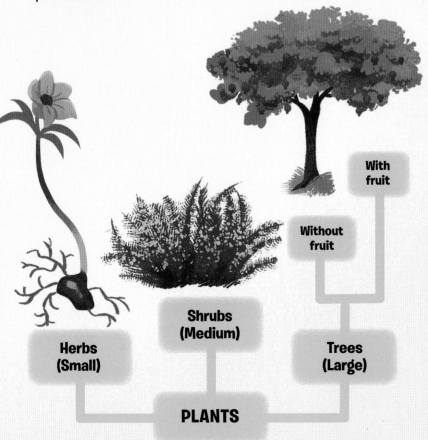

With fruit

Without fruit

Herbs (Small)

Shrubs (Medium)

Trees (Large)

PLANTS

The chain of being

Aristotle's idea of three types of "soul" suggested that animals are more advanced than plants, and humans are the most advanced of all. This was developed by Plotinus (205–270 CE) into a "chain of being" that put all living things in order, from the simplest to the most sophisticated (humans). Each plant or animal formed a link in the chain. Every organism shared at least one feature with that above and below it, fixing it in its place. This idea implied that the living world was full and perfect— everything that could exist, did exist.

Plotinus' chain of being

Human

Mammal

Bird

Simple animal

Plant

Mineral

ICE AND SEA

While people in the Middle East, China, and Greece were writing their ideas down and even recording scientific thinking, there were many cultures around the world that left no written records. We can sometimes work out the kind of scientific knowledge they had, but not how they saw this knowledge or how it fitted into their view of the world.

Out in the cold

The Thule culture began in Alaska and moved west until its people reached Greenland between 1000 and 1500 CE. They developed useful technologies for the cold areas where they lived, using knowledge that we would now call "scientific." They knew about the ways animals behaved, various physical forces, and materials and their properties.

The early Thule relied on hunting large sea mammals such as whales for food. Their homes were dug into the ground and made from whalebone and stones covered with turf. They built these homes with an underground entrance tunnel that went lower than the floor of the house before rising up to enter the living space, so that cold air would get trapped in the tunnel instead of reaching the house. They made small kayaks for hunting, and large open boats called "umiaks," which had a framework of bone or driftwood and were covered with seal or walrus skins. Oiling their boats with seal oil made them waterproof. To move on land, they used dog sleds made from driftwood with whalebone runners. They poured water over the runners to give them a coating of ice, which made the sled almost friction-free so that it moved quickly and easily.

To kill huge, heavy whales, the Thule used a "toggling" harpoon that worked with the forces of torsion, buoyancy, and drag. The barbed point of the harpoon detached and twisted into the animal, creating torsion (tension caused by twisting) and making it almost impossible for the point to slip out. The line attached to the harpoon had inflated bladders which acted as buoys (floats). These floated, creating drag (resistance) as the animal tried to swim away.

Toggle harpoon

The open sea

On the other side of the world, in steamy heat, Polynesian sailors used knowledge of the stars, sea currents, weather, and habits of birds to navigate the Pacific Ocean. Over thousands of years, they colonized the islands of the Pacific from small boats. They left no written records, but even recently, Polynesian navigators have used temporary maps made of shells and sticks to chart the currents of the ocean and guide their voyages.

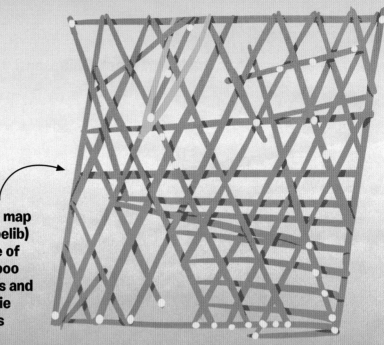

Stick map (rebbelib) made of bamboo sticks and cowrie shells

Sailors setting out for new islands took plants and animals with them so that they could set up breeding colonies and provide themselves with sustainable food in their new home.

GOLD, IMMORTALITY, AND DEATH

The earliest form of chemistry was called "alchemy." It was partly scientific and partly a mystical exploration of chemical substances. It started in China and Egypt at around the same time. In both places, alchemists tried to turn cheaper substances into gold and to find an elixir of eternal life—a potion that would make people live forever.

Fang is the earliest known woman alchemist in China. She worked in the first century BCE.

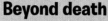

Beyond death

Alchemy probably began in China in the second century BCE, or perhaps even earlier. The first Qin emperor, Shi Huang, reportedly sent alchemists to find something which would make him immortal. He may have died after drinking a potion containing mercury, which he thought would give him eternal life—but mercury is very poisonous.

Oddly, a potion that killed someone wasn't always seen as a failure! The emperor would be enjoying eternity in the afterlife, so he would have achieved a kind of immortality after all. Emperor Shi was buried in a huge tomb, guarded by thousands of life-size terracotta warriors who were supposed to serve him in the afterlife.

Alchemy in Egypt

The earliest western book on alchemy, written in the fourth century CE, reports that the first alchemist was "Mary the Jewess." She probably worked between the first and third centuries CE in Alexandria, Egypt, though nothing is known about her for certain. Alchemy spread from Egypt into the developing Arab world. Arab alchemists perfected practical skills and made many valuable discoveries in chemistry. Equipment, substances, important techniques, and words such as "alcohol" and "alkali" that are still used today come from the Arab alchemists. The alchemist Jabir ibn Hayyān, who lived in Iraq in the ninth century CE, is sometimes called the "father of chemistry."

Arab alchemists learned how to distil liquids, a technique still used today to separate liquids with different boiling points.

Mixed-up magic

Alchemy involved some genuine chemistry: extracting, mixing, and purifying substances. But another part was mystical or magical. Different metals were thought to have characters, to be male and female, and to have mystical properties. To keep alchemy secret, texts were written in riddles, with pictures that used animals and other figures to stand for different substances and processes. Some rogue alchemists cheated people, pretending to have made gold, and this gave alchemy a bad name. Several countries passed laws banning the production of fake "gold" to protect people from being scammed.

Chinese rockets were an early use of gunpowder

Worth more than gold

Alchemists in China also made important discoveries. One of these was gunpowder, one of four great inventions that came out of ancient China. The other three inventions were paper; the magnetic compass, used for navigating; and printing with movable type.

Gunpowder was first used for fireworks, but soon became valuable for weapons. It was used to fire flaming arrows, and in early versions of hand-grenades and bombs. Although the Chinese tried to keep the recipe secret, it soon leaked out, changing the face of warfare forever.

A CONNECTED WORLD

When people move around, they carry knowledge with them, spreading and sharing ideas with other cultures. Some of the greatest thinkers of Ancient Greece visited Egypt and Turkey, picking up ideas begun in Mesopotamia and Egypt. Between 334 and 323 BCE, the Greek conqueror Alexander the Great invaded lands from Egypt to India, taking new ideas far beyond Greece. As people began to travel and trade between Europe and Asia, even as far as China, they carried knowledge and inventions with them. Much later, voyages of discovery, exploration, and invasion forged links between Europe and the Americas, finding unfamiliar plants, animals, and geology.

The start of printing in Europe in the 1400s meant that scientific knowledge could be widely shared over short and long distances. The introduction of Hindu–Arabic numerals (0–9) made calculations easier, too. In Europe, greater religious and political tolerance allowed people to question the natural world without fear of punishment. This put Europe at the forefront of scientific discovery from the 1500s.

FORGING THE FUTURE

Alchemy was only one aspect of science taken up by Arab scholars. The caliph (Muslim ruler) Harun al-Rashid (ruled 786–809 CE) founded the "House of Wisdom" in Baghdad, Iraq, as a place of learning. Here, Arab scholars collected and translated all the works they could find from the ancient Greeks and other earlier cultures. They added to them with their own expertise, laying the groundwork for the whole of modern science. The "Golden Age of Islam" lasted from the founding of the House of Wisdom until the Mongols invaded Baghdad in 1258.

House of Wisdom, Baghdad

Learning together

Ancient Greek scholars had visited the eastern Mediterranean and learned from their predecessors in Egypt and Mesopotamia. Then they had built on that knowledge. The pattern of learning from other lands was repeated as the Arabs became the most accomplished scientists in the world. They made progress in optics (the study of light and lenses), astronomy, chemistry (through alchemy), medicine, and anatomy.

Camera obscura

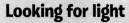

Ibn al-Haytham

Looking for light

Around 1011, Ibn al-Haytham explained vision in terms of light coming into the eye. Before this, people thought the eye sent out beams to capture an image of the objects we see. Al-Haytham also said that light travels in straight lines, and he described the "camera obscura."

In a camera obscura, light rays passing through a small hole cross over, making an inverted image on a screen. This visible image can only be explained if light travels through the hole to project on the screen—it can't be the result of rays coming from the eye.

Arab work on optics included making glass lenses that changed the focus of light. Arab scientists probably made more progress in optics than in any other area.

Not only al-Haytham's discoveries but also his methods were important. He stressed the importance of testing ideas with experiments, using something similar to the modern scientific method.

Blazing the trail

The world in which the highly talented Arab scientists lived didn't encourage the kind of free thinking and exploration needed for great scientific breakthroughs to take place. Science relies on the belief that the Universe follows rational physical rules, and that humans can eventually discover and understand those rules. It needs a space in which anything can be questioned and discussed without fear of punishment and without being restricted by religious beliefs or laws. That kind of intellectual freedom didn't exist anywhere at the time, but it would emerge a few hundred years later in Europe. The Arab scientists couldn't make the leap to modern science, but they made it possible for future generations to do so.

Quadrant

Astrolabe

Arab astronomers used tools such as a quadrant and an astrolabe to observe and model the positions of planets and stars.

CHALLENGING THE ANCIENTS

The Arab scientists paved the way for modern science by investigating and eventually challenging the ideas they took from earlier cultures. As they worked with ancient ideas, they found areas where those ideas didn't work well enough. They added new observations and raised doubts that made major discoveries possible—even inevitable.

Arab scientists went beyond ancient ideas in two particularly important areas: astronomy and medicine. Ptolemy's work on astronomy and Galen's work on medicine had been accepted without question for centuries, yet both men had made crucial errors.

Looking to the stars

Muslims pray at precise times of day, so an accurate calendar was important in the early Arab world. A calendar relies on accurate astronomical observations and calculations, so Arab scientists put a lot of effort into perfecting these. Arab astronomers made tools for observing the stars and planets that revolutionized astronomy. These included celestial globes (globes that show the stars in the sky), astrolabes for calculating the positions of planets and the Sun, and quadrants for measuring the height above the horizon of a planet, a star, or the Sun.

Beginning with the work of al-Khwarizmi in 830 CE, Arab astronomers made new measurements and used improved mathematics to go beyond the discoveries of the Persians, Indians, and Greeks. They calculated Earth's circumference and the tilt of its axis more accurately than ever before. They found and discussed problems in Ptolemy's account of the solar system, adjusting his method for working out positions and dates to make it more accurate. Some astronomers suggested that Earth turns on its axis.

But no astronomer went as far as saying that Ptolemy was wrong, and that the planets go around the Sun, not around Earth.

Treating the whole human

The Arabs introduced proper medical training for their physicians and established hospitals with a high level of care that treated mental as well as physical illness. One of the greatest medical figures was Ibn Sina (980-1037), who treated the whole body, combining pharmacology (drug-based treatments) with diet and concern for mental health. The surgeon Abu Al-Qasim Al-Zahrawi designed new medical instruments and sutures (stitches) to hold wounds together, and wrote medical texts that would be used for hundreds of years afterward.

Body of knowledge

Skilled Arab surgeons developed new instruments for precise work, many of which are still used today, and learned a great deal about the human body and how to treat it. Some carried out experiments and even dissections (cutting open a dead body to investigate the inside), though dissection was not always legal. Dissection enabled people to see how parts of the body work together. The physician al-Rhazi (c.864–925 or 935) tested mercury on animals to find out the fatal (deadly) dose, and in the thirteenth century, Peter of Spain described an experimental method for testing whether a medicine works.

Ibn al-Nafis (1213–1288) described the circulation of the blood through the lungs 300 years before it was explained in Europe.

A NEW ASTRONOMY

Between the Golden Age of Islamic science and the sixteenth century, astronomy didn't change much, but the work of the Arabs and Greeks was translated into Latin. Latin, the language of the Romans, was used across Europe for religious and official documents and for scholarship.

With these translations, European scientists had all the knowledge of the past at their fingertips.

Around the Sun

Although the Arab scientists found faults in Ptolemy's geocentric model, they didn't replace it. That didn't happen until the sixteenth and seventeenth centuries, when a revolution in astronomy in the West finally overturned old ideas. In 1543, the Polish astronomer Copernicus suggested that all the planets orbit a central Sun, leaving only the Moon going around Earth. But this model didn't produce better predictions than the latest version of Ptolemy's system, developed by Arab astronomers, and it contradicted tradition and the view of the Catholic Church. Most people ignored it. The Danish astronomer Tycho Brahe suggested another possibility, with the other planets going around the Sun, but the Sun still going around Earth, trailing all the other planets. There was no advantage to this scheme, either.

Imperfect orbits

Brahe was the last great astronomer who didn't use a telescope. He recorded thousands of observations, and passed them on to his assistant Johannes Kepler when he died. Using Brahe's observations, Kepler realized that Copernicus had made an important mistake: he'd assumed that the planets had perfectly circular orbits. In 1609, Kepler published his own system with the planets moving in elliptical (oval) orbits around the Sun. This time, the predicted orbits matched how the planets actually move.

SUN

Copernicus put the Sun at the middle of the solar system and all the planets in orbit around it.

Changing heavens

A lot happened between Copernicus and Kepler. First, a supernova appeared in 1572. A supernova is an exploding star, so bright that it's visible even in daytime. This alarmed astronomers who believed that the heavens were unchanging. Then in 1577, a bright comet appeared. With careful calculations, Brahe showed that it was outside Earth's atmosphere. Previously, people had thought that comets were a feature of the weather. Proving that comets were outside the atmosphere also showed that the heavens are not fixed forever.

Tycho Brahe's observatory on an island in Denmark.

Galileo Galilei

Worlds away

Astronomy was transformed by the invention of the telescope in 1608. The next year, Italian scientist Galileo Galilei turned his telescope to the sky and made some astonishing discoveries— that the planets are other worlds; the fuzzy band of the Milky Way is millions of stars; the Moon has craters and mountains; and Jupiter has moons of its own. Galileo's work supported Kepler's model of the Sun in the middle of the solar system. The Church tried to stop anyone from teaching that Earth goes around the Sun, but in the end they failed. Isaac Newton's work on gravity, published in the 1680s, proved that Kepler had been right.

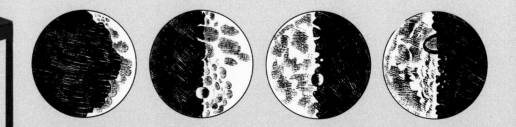

Galileo's drawings of craters on the Moon overturned the idea that the Moon is perfectly smooth.

INSIDE THE BODY

Just as Arab scientists found faults in Ptolemy's model of the Universe, they also found faults in Galen's medical writings. But they didn't directly overturn the traditional texts. Arab doctors made great advances in medicine, especially in treatment and surgery, but modern medicine needed a different approach—that started by rejecting Galen's ideas.

Treatments such as making patients vomit or cutting them so that they bled often made matters worse, rather than better.

In good humor

Galen's work was based on the Greek theory of humors, explained by Hippocrates around 400 BCE, and on his own observations and dissections. Unfortunately, he often dissected animals and he assumed that the human body would be the same, when it's actually different in some important ways. Many medical treatments tried to "rebalance" the bodily humors (blood, phlegm, yellow bile, and black bile) using methods such as bloodletting, hot baths, or potions to make the patient vomit.

Under the skin

Real progress in understanding the human body only came when people began to look carefully inside it. In 1315, the Italian physician Mondino de Luzzi carried out a public dissection of a dead body for his students and other spectators. The following year, he wrote the first dissection manual.

The Belgian doctor Andreas Vesalius felt strongly that knowledge of the body must be based on direct experience of dissecting human corpses. His careful dissections showed how the body's internal structures fit together and gave clues as to how they work. He published an illustrated book on the human body in 1543—the same year that Copernicus contradicted Ptolemy's model of the solar system.

Vesalius's illustrations of muscles and bones showed how the body works as a mechanical system.

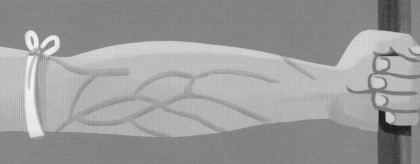

Heart's blood

Although the Egyptian physician Ibn al-Nafis had worked out how blood circulates between the lungs and the heart, his work wasn't known in Europe. William Harvey described the full circulation of the blood in detail in 1628. This showed that Galen was wrong when he taught that the liver produces the blood.

Harvey showed that if blood is prevented from returning to the heart by tying a band around the arm, blood below the band builds up, making the veins swell.

The body as machine

The work of Vesalius and Harvey began a new way of thinking about the body as a mechanical system. The body has parts that work as levers and tubes with flowing liquid that follow the laws of physics. Some parts were hard to work out. People could not decide whether digestion was chemical or mechanical. Nerves were a puzzle, too—they were once thought to be hollow, but people could find no evidence for this. The French thinker and mathematician René Descartes was prompted to think of the body as a kind of mechanism after he saw mechanical fountains and automata (automated models). But he still struggled with the idea of the spirit or soul. He couldn't see how the physical body could interact with a non-physical mind or soul.

In the seventeenth century, René Descartes wrote about the link between the body and the brain. He thought nerves were like cords: if you stand too close to a fire, the nerves would "tug" at a gland in the brain, and the brain would send air to the muscles to inflate them and cause them to move.

The surgeon Amboise Paré made a mechanical hand for an injured soldier, using the idea that muscles and bones work together like parts in a machine.

MICRO-WORLDS

Until a little over 400 years ago, no one could see anything much smaller than the width of a human hair. Then, around 1590, a Dutch lensmaker put two glass lenses into a tube and made the first microscope. This invention revealed unimagined wonders of miniature life and changed our view of the world for ever.

Starting small

The very first microscopes could magnify to around x9, meaning that an object looked nine times its actual size. Microscopes were a novelty at first, used for looking at small insects such as fleas and beetles. This was amusing and informative, but "flea glasses" weren't put to serious scientific use for another 70 years.

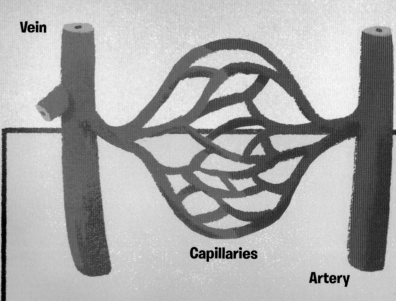

Vein

Capillaries

Artery

Making connections

The Italian anatomist Marcello Malpighi made the first important scientific discovery with a microscope in 1661. He saw the capillaries—the tiny blood vessels that connect the arteries and veins, allowing blood to circulate around the body. When Harvey described circulation in 1628, he couldn't explain how blood moved from the arteries, which carry it away from the heart, into the veins which carry it back. Capillaries made that connection, showing that Harvey's description of circulation was correct.

Hooke's microscope

Seeing cells

Soon, the microscope revealed more wonders. In 1665, English scientist Robert Hooke published *Micrographia*, showing objects he had seen through his microscope. The most famous was a flea, an animal familiar to everyone back then, but never before seen in such detail. Hooke made the first drawings of a microorganism —a fungus called *Mucor*—and of cells. Seeing that a slice of cork was divided into areas that looked like the small rooms, or cells, that monks lived in, Hooke named the compartments "cells." They're now known to be the components of all living things.

Life in miniature

So far, people had only looked closely at known organisms. That changed with Antonie van Leeuwenhoek in the 1670s. He revealed the teeming life of the microscopic world, finding thousands of microorganisms everywhere he looked. A Dutch cloth merchant, Leeuwenhoek began making lenses to look at the fine threads of the fabrics he worked with, but soon discovered something far more fascinating. He was the first person to see bacteria, finding a whole world of tiny living things in drops of cloudy water. He examined bacteria from his mouth, as well as muscle cells, sperm, and blood cells. He called the microbes he saw "animalcules," meaning "tiny animals". His microscopes were miniature hand-held devices which had far greater magnification than others available at the time.

Modern microscopes

Today's microscopes can magnify specimens to thousands of times their original size. Electron microscopes, which work by bouncing electrons off an object, are so powerful that they can see viruses and even single molecules.

Modern electron microscopes are very powerful.

THE AGE OF EXPERIMENT

Throughout the Middle Ages, scientists used a method called "scholasticism." It was based in the confidence people had in earlier scholars, such as Aristotle, Ptolemy, and Galen. As people became more confident that they could work things out for themselves, a new method emerged.

Ways of knowing

In 1620, the English philosopher Roger Bacon challenged the old way of doing science. He said that scientific knowledge didn't need to come from books, but could be gained directly from the world around us, through careful observation and experiments. Bacon used a method called "induction" that involved looking at evidence from the real world and trying to find explanations for what he saw. He suggested designing an experiment to test a hypothesis (a suggested explanation). The experiment should be a "fair test," changing only one condition at a time, so that any difference in the results can be linked to that change. This is the basis of the modern scientific method. Many important experiments followed in the seventeenth century.

Testing trees

The Belgian scientist Jan Baptist van Helmont (1580–1646) assumed that plants took most of the chemicals they use to grow from soil. He tested his idea with an experiment. He weighed a willow sapling, planted it in a pot with a known weight of soil, and watered it, keeping the pot covered so that nothing else could fall in. After five years, he weighed the tree and the soil again.

He found that the tree had gained 74 kg (167 lb) but the soil had lost only 57 g (2 oz). He concluded that the tree had grown almost entirely from water. This isn't correct—it was taking carbon dioxide from the air, too—but his experiment was rigorous and his conclusion fitted with the results. It was reasonable given the level of knowledge at the time.

Water

2.3 kg (5 lb)	90 kg (198 lb, 4oz)	5 years	76.3 kg (167 lb)	89.9 kg (198 lb, 2oz)
Willow sapling	Soil	later	Willow tree	Soil

Santorio and his weighing chair

Eating experiments

The Italian scientist Santorio Santorio (1561–1636) investigated his own body in the first quantitative experiment in physiology (how bodies function). Over a period of 30 years, he used a special "weighing chair" to record how his weight changed as he ate, drank, and released body waste. He found that for every 3.6 kg (8 lb) of food he ate, he only excreted 1.4 kg (3 lb), but he didn't grow heavier. He concluded that his body must be losing chemicals through his skin in "insensible perspiration," or through breathing.

Spallanzani

Discovering digestion

Lazzaro Spallanzani (1729-1799) experimented on animals to investigate digestion. People were unsure whether digestion was a chemical or mechanical process. By getting birds to swallow capsules of meat which he then pulled back up their throat, Spallanzani showed that the meat was partially dissolved. This proved that digestion is at least partly chemical.

IN THE AIR

Air is all around us, yet we can't see it. We know we need it—people suffocate if they don't have air—and we can see its effects, for example, when trees move in the wind. The investigation of gases, such as those in the air, began in the seventeenth century.

Can there be nothing?

Early Greek thinkers had wondered whether there can be somewhere entirely empty, without even air. We now call this a vacuum. Aristotle thought it was impossible for "nothing" to exist—partly because it sounds illogical (nothing can't be something). Others said that there must be empty space for things to move.

The question was settled by Evangelista Torricelli in 1643. He made the first barometer, a tool which measures air pressure. He filled a tube with mercury, then turned it over into a flask of mercury. A gap appeared at the top of the column as a little of the mercury flowed out of the tube, leaving a vacuum.

The pressure of air on the mercury in the dish controls how far up the tube the mercury goes. When air pressure is high, it pushes down on the mercury so that more rises up the tube. When air pressure is low, the mercury in the tube falls.

In Torricelli's barometer, the level of the mercury in the tube settles where air pressure (pushing it up) and gravity (pulling it down) are balanced.

Magdeburg hemispheres

The power of air

In 1654, Otto von Guericke spectacularly demonstrated a vacuum. He made two hemispheres (half spheres) of metal that fitted together perfectly, then pumped all the air out of them. He tethered a team of horses to each hemisphere and used them to try to pull the metal spheres apart. The pressure of air outside forcing the hemispheres together was too great for the horses to pull against, and the hemispheres remained stuck together.

What's in the air?

It's not immediately obvious that the air around us is a mixture of different gases, but this became clear when chemists began to experiment with gases. In 1774, the English chemist Joseph Priestley showed in an experiment that both a mouse and a burning candle use up the same element of the air. If they're placed in a closed jar together, eventually the candle goes out and the mouse dies. If he put a living plant in the jar, though, the mouse lived, and the candle continued to burn.

Breath of life

The link between the mouse and the plant was finally explained in the 1770s. The Dutch scientist Jan Ingenhousz captured the bubbles of gas from an underwater plant and showed that they were the gas needed by burning candles and breathing mice—oxygen. A photosynthesising plant takes carbon dioxide from the air, and water from the soil or water it grows in, and releases oxygen. This exchange of gases powers all life on Earth.

Oxygen

PHOTOSYNTHESIS

Oxygen

Sunlight

Carbon dioxide

Water

UNFAMILIAR WORLDS

Between the 1490s and the late 1800s, European explorers and invaders went to places they'd never been before, including the Americas, Australia, and deep into India and Africa. Their voyages often ended badly for the people already living in these areas as Europeans slaughtered or enslaved them, took their land, and seized their resources. But for science, exploration revealed unfamiliar plants and animals, and changed how we think about the natural world.

PEOPLE OF SCIENCE

Maria Sybilla Merian was a German naturalist and artist. She was one of the first people to study insects in detail, investigating their metamorphosis and the plants they lived on. She went to Suriname (in South America) in 1699 to study, describe, and classify the animals and plants she found there. She used native American names for the species she described.

Animals across borders

Imagine being a European explorer, visiting Australia for the first time and seeing marsupials such as kangaroos and koalas. Or being a native American and seeing the horses brought over the sea by colonists. These completely unfamiliar animals were a challenge to people who believed all living things were already known. We don't know what the native Americans made of horses when they first saw them, but we do know that Europeans recorded the new species they encountered with astonishment.

Maria Sybilla Merian

Working together

Some expeditions took professional zoologists and botanists to record their discoveries. These experts often worked closely with local people to find, record, name, and sort plants and animals. The expertise of local people was crucial to the work of European scientists, but it was rarely credited and their names are mostly unknown today.

Mammals

In 1758, Linnaeus Linnaeus divided animals into six main classes—"quadrupeds" (mammals); birds; amphibians and reptiles; fish; insects; and worms and mollusks.

Birds

Amphibians and reptiles

From chain to classification

In Christian Europe, people traditionally thought of living things in a "Chain of Being" based on the work of Plotinus (see page 41) that put them in an order fixed by God and already complete. The chain couldn't be prised apart to add thousands of newly discovered organisms. A new system was needed, and the Swedish naturalist Carl Linnaeus provided it in the 1750s.

Fish

First, he named two "kingdoms," plants and animals. Then he divided organisms into classes based on similarities between them—such as having four legs and producing milk for their young (animals now called mammals). Then he divided classes into orders. Below orders, there were two categories, genus and species, which gave the organism its two-part Latin name. So bears have the genus *Ursus*, and particular types of bears have their own species name, such as brown bears, *Ursus arctos*. Linnaeus focused on how organisms look and behave when grouping them. This led him to class whales and bats as mammals, while previously people thought whales were fish and bats were birds.

Worms and mollusks

Linnaeus recognized at least 87 different forms of leaf.

Insects

EXPLORATION AND DISCOVERY

Mary Anning excavating an Ichthyosaur fossil.

From the eighteenth century, people came to understand more of the hidden science of matter, energy, and the distant past. Discoveries about the nature of light, electricity, heat, other types of energy, atoms, and radioactivity were not always of practical use as they emerged, but they are the basis of our modern world. As the technologies of the Industrial Revolution developed, people dug canals and coal mines. When they cut through the rock, they found that the story of Earth itself is far from static. They discovered fossils of long dead animals, nothing like any animal then living, and they worked out that Earth has changed and is still changing. Science had been freed from old errors by the work of scientists in the sixteenth, seventeenth, and eighteenth centuries, and now it raced ahead into the future.

ROCK OF AGES

Geology is the study of Earth, including its rocks, water, and climate, the processes that have shaped it, and how it formed. For thousands of years, people explained geological processes through myths and religion. Earthquakes and volcanic eruptions were blamed on angry gods, and the formation of Earth was described in creation myths. People began to think more scientifically about rocks and the history of our planet in the late 1700s.

Making rocks

The Persian scholar Ibn-Sena (c.970–1037) suggested that rock could be produced by either water or heat. It could grow from water, as when the rocky spikes of stalactites grow from dripping water. Or it could be formed by heat, as when clay hardens as it dries. He said that once Earth had been entirely covered with water, and more land had emerged as it dried out. This explained why fossils of sea creatures were found on land. He was right that once there was more water and less land.

The English geologist Charles Lyell noticed holes created by sea creatures in ancient Roman columns. He realized that this meant the sea level had risen and then fallen again since the columns were built.

Changing Earth

The Greek thinker Xenophanes (570–480 BCE) used the existence of fossilized marine organisms inland to support his view that Earth goes through alternating periods of being wet and dry. Much later, Shen Kuo (1031–1095) suggested that Earth's surface and climate had changed over long periods, after he found fossilized bamboo in an area of China where bamboo no longer grew.

Shen Kuo

Fossilized marine animal

Fossilized bamboo

Digging into the past

As industry expanded in the eighteenth and nineteenth centuries, people cut canals to move goods by boat and dug mines for coal to power machinery. Excavations cut vertically through layers of rock and across wide areas, revealing rocks beneath the surface in different places. James Hutton, a farmer and businessman interested in geology, saw that rock is laid down in layers, called "strata," one forming on top of another. The strata might be disturbed, making "discontinuities" such as tipped-over layers, but where they are not disturbed the oldest rock is always lowest. He decided that Earth is immeasurably old and has been constantly reshaped by very slow geological processes ... which are still happening!

Ancient Earth

Hutton's ideas were made popular by Charles Lyell who went further in saying that mountains, lakes, valleys, coastlines, and even the climate have been forged over thousands of years by geological processes such as volcanic eruptions and earthquakes.

Fast or slow?

Hutton's idea of slow, steady processes is called "uniformitarianism." Other scientists took a different view that became known as "catastrophism." The French naturalist Georges Cuvier, who worked on fossils, had decided that sudden, occasional catastrophes during Earth's history had caused many animals to become extinct (die out). These catastrophes were, he thought, geological events such as widespread floods.

James Hutton

Smith published his geological maps in 1815.

All in order

In 1799, William Smith began mapping 175,000 square km (109,000 square mi) of Britain. He noticed that different fossils occur in different strata. He realized that he could use fossils to identify the same strata in different places. Today, key fossils are used to work out the age of rocks.

STRANGE STONES

People have been finding fossils for at least 2,500 years, and probably much longer. When they thought about them scientifically, it became clear that they're relics of dead creatures. But when people found fossils of completely unfamiliar animals that no longer existed, it was another challenge to the idea of a perfect natural world, created and finished by a god.

Dead but not gone

In the tenth century, Ibn-Sena suggested that a kind of "petrifying" (stone-forming) substance had turned ancient creatures to stone. But not everyone connected fossils to living things. One common idea was that they grew naturally in the ground. Another was that if "seeds" of living things fell on the ground, rocks could grow to look like the organism the seeds came from.

The fish in the rock

Modern fossil science (paleontology) began with the Danish anatomist Niels Stensen (Steno), in 1666. Examining the body of a giant shark, he noticed that its teeth were similar to common, triangular "tongue stones." He realized the stones were really teeth from long-dead sharks. He suggested that "corpuscles" (molecules) of the teeth had been replaced by stone over a long time, and more rock had formed above them, trapping the teeth inside rock.

The North American mastodon was similar to the Siberian mammoth, and related to modern elephants.

American elephants

Steno's fossilized teeth looked the same as modern shark teeth, but from the late 1700s, people started finding fossils that had no living counterparts. This challenged the idea that nature doesn't change. In 1739, French soldiers in North America found large animal bones near the Ohio River. More bones were found and sent to Europe, where scientists puzzled over them, wondering if they were from an unknown animal that could still be living undiscovered. In 1796, the French naturalist Georges Cuvier realized that the bones were from a type of elephant, and similar to those being dug up in Siberia, Russia.

Plesiosaur fossil

Pterosaur

First pterosaur fossil

Plesiosaur

Flying and swimming

Mastodons are recognizable as elephants—but the real challenge was still to come. When Cosimo Collini found the first pterosaur, he thought it was a marine animal, but Cuvier showed in 1801 that it flew instead. A pterosaur isn't like a bird. It has teeth in its mouth, a bony tail, and claws on its wings. From 1811, fossil hunter Mary Anning found ichthyosaurs and plesiosaurs, both giant marine reptiles. Nothing like any of these animals exists today. People finally had to accept that living things change and some die out.

Lost worlds

More surprises were to come. In 1815, the bones of *Megalosaurus* were found in England. By 1842, three different types of giant reptile were known, and English scientist Richard Owen named them "dinosaurs." Working out what these long-dead animals looked like while they were alive was difficult, and the first reconstructions of dinosaurs looked nothing like modern reconstructions.

Megalosaurus

Early reconstruction

Modern interpretation

THE SPARK OF LIFE

Have you ever got a little shock from static electricity when touching a metal door handle? Static electricity was noticed by the ancient Greeks and demonstrated scientifically in the seventeenth century. For electricity to become useful, though, it had to be stored or generated (produced) as needed.

Gray staged demonstrations in which he charged a boy with static electricity and showed him attracting scraps of paper that floated up to him.

Jumping sparks

In the 1660s, Otto von Geuricke built a device to store static electricity. When he rotated and rubbed a ball of sulfur, an electric charge built up on it, and scraps of paper or feathers would stick to it. From the 1720s, the English scientist Stephen Gray found that some materials would conduct static electricity and could be used to move it from one place to another.

Power in a jar

Gray's "flying boy" was fun to watch, but not useful. The first device to store electricity for later use was the Leyden jar, invented in 1745. It consisted of a jar part-filled with water and with a thick metal rod held in it. The jar was charged with static electricity. It was widely used for experiments and tricks—showing sparks carried through wire over rivers, or killing unfortunate small animals.

Leyden jar

In America, Benjamin Franklin showed that lightning is an electric charge. In 1752, he flew a kite in a thunderstorm, charging a metal key hung from the kite's wet string. He stored the electricity in a Leyden jar to use for experiments.

From frogs to batteries

One popular demonstration involved passing an electric charge through a row of people and seeing them all jump. In 1791, Luigi Galvani discovered why the people jumped. He found that an electric shock makes the legs of a dead frog twitch. He also discovered that he didn't even need to provide electricity—just bringing two metals, copper and iron, to frog legs made them jump. Acid in the frog's body reacted with the metals to make electricity flow through the leg and make the muscles contract. Later, people would realize that the nerves carry electrical impulses to make muscles move.

Italian anatomist Galvani found that in a thunderstorm, frog legs hung on a metal fence would twitch.

Alessandro Volta found that he could make electricity flow without a frog. He made the first battery in 1800 by layering paper or fabric soaked in salt water between disks of copper and zinc. Wires attached to the top and bottom of this device could carry the electricity away.

Electricity put to use

In 1820, Hans Christian Ørsted showed that when electricity flows through a wire, a magnetic field appears around the wire. The next year, Michael Faraday made the first electric motor, making a wire rotate around a magnet. Electrical energy was changed into kinetic (movement) energy. In 1831, when he showed that electricity can be made by turning a metal disk between the poles of a magnet, the age of useful electricity could begin.

WHAT MAKES MATTER?

The ancient idea that matter is made by mixing four elements in different proportions survived for thousands of years. The alchemists had slightly different ideas, but still thought that there were only a few basic ingredients for all matter. One idea was that everything is made from mixes of gold and mercury. This would make it possible to change other metals into gold by removing the mercury.

Back to basics

As chemists discovered more gases in the air, the idea of what makes up matter became more challenging—air couldn't be a single element. In 1789, the French chemist Lavoisier published a new scheme—that all matter is made of a limited set of basic ingredients, either alone or combined. These ingredients are now called the chemical elements. Lavoisier listed 33 elements. Some of these are still recognized as elements, some are now known to be compounds (two or more elements combined), and others aren't even physical substances. For example, he listed gold and oxygen, which are both elements, but also quicklime, which is a compound of calcium and oxygen, and heat, which isn't a substance at all.

As well as the idea of the elements, Lavoisier showed that substances need oxygen to burn, that water is a compound of two gases, oxygen and hydrogen, and that there is always the same mass of chemicals before and after any reaction—nothing can be lost or gained.

Lavoisier's wife, Marie Anne Pierrette Paulze, helped him with his chemical work.

Among Lavoisier's "elements" he included heat, light, and the compound quicklime (calcium oxide).

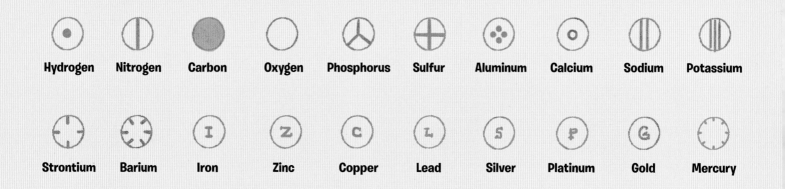

| Hydrogen | Nitrogen | Carbon | Oxygen | Phosphorus | Sulfur | Aluminum | Calcium | Sodium | Potassium |
| Strontium | Barium | Iron | Zinc | Copper | Lead | Silver | Platinum | Gold | Mercury |

Eternal atoms

The English chemist John Dalton took on Lavoisier's idea and explained how it works at the tiniest level. In 1800, he stated that all matter is made up of tiny particles that can't be further divided, called atoms. Each chemical element has its own unique type of atom. The differences between these atoms account for the differences between different types of matter. Compounds are made by combining atoms of different elements, always in the same proportions to gain the same substances. In chemical reactions, atoms can be combined, separated from each other, or rearranged—but they are never created or destroyed.

Dalton used different symbols for the atoms of different chemical elements.

Dmitri Mendeleev

All in order

During the nineteenth century, chemists found more and more elements. Some people tried to put them in order, often based on their relative weights. The most successful attempt came from the Russian chemist Dmitri Mendeleev in 1869. He noticed that if he listed the elements in increasing order of weight, some characteristics of the substances repeated regularly (periodically). He drew up a table of the elements in order, even predicting where he thought undiscovered elements should fit in. Some of these elements were soon discovered, convincing many people that he was right. The modern periodic table of the elements is based on Mendeleev's original work and has 118 elements.

All substances are made of chemicals now recognized as elements, including (clockwise from top) gold, carbon, chlorine, sulfur, and mercury.

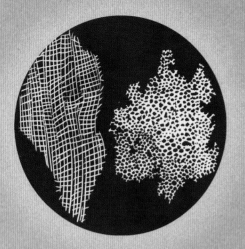

CELL THEORY

When Robert Hooke first saw cells with his microscope in 1665, he didn't know how important they are. He just saw the walls of dead cells in a piece of dry cork, with nothing inside them—but in living organisms, cells are far more complicated. They are the active units of all living things.

A world of cells

More than 150 years after Hooke first saw cells, two German scientists realized that all plants and animals have cells. Indeed, all living bodies are made up of cells of different types with some basic similarities. Matthias Schleiden was a botanist who worked on plant cells. He had dinner with Theodor Schwann, a physician, and described the cells he had seen and how new plant cells grew from existing plant cells. Schwann realized that he had seen something very similar in the animals he studied. The pair did more work, and recognized that both plants and animals are made up of cells.

Leaf cells in a plant have a simple structure with a clear nucleus and cell wall. The nucleus was first named by Robert Brown in 1831.

In 1839, Schwann published a book setting out the basics of cell theory in three points: (1) that all living things are made of cells; (2) cells are individual working units as well as building blocks of whole organisms; and (3) cells carry out all the functions of life in organisms.

In a sponge, one type of cell has a flagellum (tail-like structure) which wafts water through the sponge, while another type can absorb food from the water.

Cells make more cells

One of the greatest discoveries was that cells make new cells. This, finally, would overturn the idea of "spontaneous generation"—that simple life forms could come into being from non-living matter. This belief led people to think that maggots just appeared in old meat, or even mice in sacks of corn. In 1852, the Polish scientist Robert Remak explained that all cells come from other cells, made by dividing an existing cell. Another Polish scientist, Rudolf Virchow, popularized this idea just three years later. The basis of modern cell theory was then in place—that cells are the building blocks of all life, and all cells come from the division of existing cells.

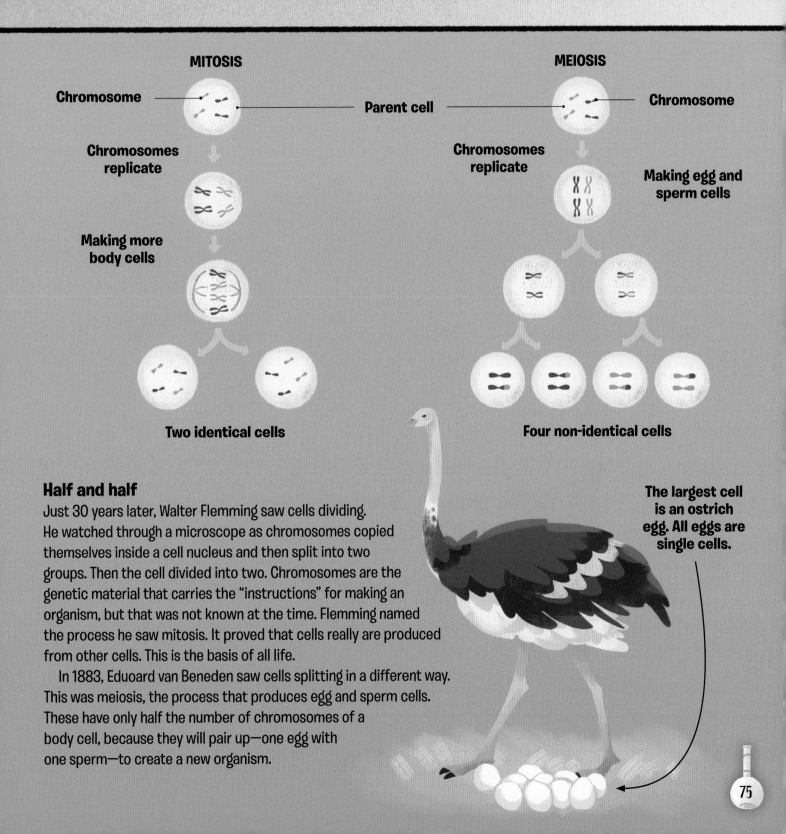

MITOSIS

Chromosome — Parent cell — Chromosome **MEIOSIS**

Chromosomes replicate

Chromosomes replicate

Making egg and sperm cells

Making more body cells

Two identical cells

Four non-identical cells

Half and half

Just 30 years later, Walter Flemming saw cells dividing. He watched through a microscope as chromosomes copied themselves inside a cell nucleus and then split into two groups. Then the cell divided into two. Chromosomes are the genetic material that carries the "instructions" for making an organism, but that was not known at the time. Flemming named the process he saw mitosis. It proved that cells really are produced from other cells. This is the basis of all life.

In 1883, Eduoard van Beneden saw cells splitting in a different way. This was meiosis, the process that produces egg and sperm cells. These have only half the number of chromosomes of a body cell, because they will pair up—one egg with one sperm—to create a new organism.

The largest cell is an ostrich egg. All eggs are single cells.

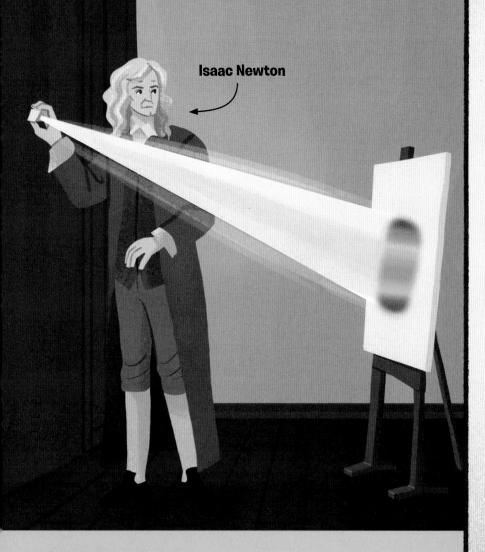

Isaac Newton

MAKING LIGHT WORK

Light has puzzled scientists for centuries. It seems to move instantaneously, it doesn't weigh anything, and it can be manipulated with lenses and mirrors. People wondered whether its speed really was infinite, whether it was made of particles or waves ("rays"), and whether it should be counted as a substance. Lavoisier included it in his list of elements.

Particles or waves?

The English physicist and mathematician Isaac Newton studied light in the 1660s. He split white light into a spectrum using a glass prism and recombined it, showing that white light is composed of a range from red to violet. Newton said light is made of particles, which he called "corpuscles."

Thomas Young thought differently. In 1801, he carried out a famous experiment, passing light through two slits to cast a series of dark and light bands on a screen. This showed waves of light interfering with each other, like waves in water colliding and mixing. If light was particles, there would only be light opposite the slits. Today, scientists say that light behaves like both particles and waves.

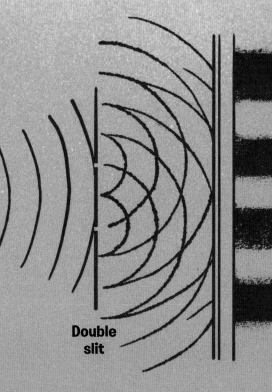

Light

Single slit

Double slit

Fast, faster, fastest

If you turn on a light, you don't have to wait for the light to reach the corners of the room—so it moves fast. But does it have a finite speed? Galileo first tried to measure the speed of light in the seventeenth century. He and his assistant stood on two hills. One would uncover a light, and the other uncovered his own light as soon as he saw it. However, all Galileo measured was the speed of his reactions, because light travels far too fast for this experiment.

Ole Römer finally measured the speed of light in 1676. Römer had been timing eclipses of Jupiter's moon Io. He found that when Earth was closest to Jupiter, a predicted eclipse came early, and when Earth was farthest from Jupiter it came late. He realized the difference was in how long light took to reach Earth. When Jupiter was close to Earth, he saw the eclipse sooner because light had less distance to travel. He worked out that light takes 22 minutes to cross Earth's orbit, giving a speed of 211,000 km per second (131,000 mi per second). The correct value is 299,000 km per second (186,000 mi per second).

Io   Jupiter

As sunlight passes through gases in the Sun's own atmosphere, some light is absorbed by elements in the atmosphere

Continuous spectrum

Absorption spectrum—light absorbed by an element

Emission spectrum—light given out by an element

Light and dark

In 1814, Joseph von Fraunhofer noticed dark lines in the spectrum of firelight. He found similar dark lines in the spectrum of sunlight and of starlight. More than 40 years later, Robert Bunsen and Gustav Kircher explained that the dark lines appear where light of a particular wavelength has been absorbed by a substance between our eyes and the light's source. Testing different chemical elements in a flame, they worked out which elements produced which black lines. From there, they could work out which elements are present in the atmosphere of stars.

LIVING AND CHANGING

The discovery of unfamiliar, extinct animals such as plesiosaurs, pterosaurs, and then dinosaurs forced scientists to change their ideas about the natural world being fixed. Finding out how and why organisms change or die out took a long time, though. The first steps toward solving the puzzle came in the second half of the nineteenth century, but the pieces weren't all put together for a few more decades.

Accepting change

Although Europeans in the nineteenth century were reluctant to accept that the natural world changes constantly, earlier thinkers were comfortable with the idea. In ancient Greece, Anaximander said that humans came from fish, and Taoist philosophers in ancient China, such as Zhuang Zhou (c.369–286 BCE), believed that organisms could change whenever conditions made it necessary. The resistance of Europeans was based on the idea that God had created all animals as finished species, and had made humankind separately to rule over them.

Sea change

The naturalist Charles Darwin went around the world as the scientist on a ship called HMS *Beagle* in 1831–1836.

On the trip, he saw unfamiliar landscapes and new plants and animals. The landscapes convinced him that Lyell was right about Earth having a long history of steady change. He applied the same ideas to the natural world, writing up his ideas in *On the Origin of Species*, published in 1859.

Charles Darwin

Darwin explained that if an animal is born with slight changes to its body that make it better suited to its living conditions, it will survive and pass on the changes to the next generation. If changes make it less well suited, it's less likely to breed and pass on its characteristics. Over a very long time, species change so that they are well suited ("fit") for the conditions they live in. When those conditions change, different characteristics might be more useful, and organisms change again.

Cactus finch (eats cactus fruits and flowers)

Large ground finch (eats seeds)

Woodpecker finch (eats insects)

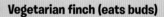

Vegetarian finch (eats buds)

Darwin described finches that live on the Galapagos Islands. On each island, finches have adapted to eat different types of food, and their beaks have changed to suit.

The first generation each have a purple and a white allele, and grow purple flowers. In the second generation, a few will inherit two white alleles and grow white flowers.

Parent generation

First generation

Second generation

From parent to child

Although Darwin knew that characteristics pass from one generation to the next, he didn't know how. Just a few years later, the monk Gregor Mendel investigated inherited traits (characteristics) in pea plants. He discovered that there are reliable patterns in inheritance and worked out that there are two markers (now called alleles) for inherited traits. One is often dominant, meaning that it will show up in the organism if it's present at all. The other is recessive and will only appear if both alleles are the same. He found that if a pure-bred purple and a pure-bred white pea plant are crossed, all the first generation are purple. They each have one allele for purple and one for white, but as the purple is dominant, the flowers are always purple. If two of these hybrids are crossed, most are purple, but a few have white flowers.

ALL KINDS OF ENERGY

Most chemists of the nineteenth century thought that heat was a type of matter which they called "caloric," and which Lavoisier had listed as an element. The flow of heat from one object to another was explained as the movement of caloric between things.

Heat in motion

Heat was first explained by the English physicist James Joule in 1843. He saw it as the result of moving particles. When a substance is heated, this provides energy to its particles, making them vibrate. People rejected his idea at first—partly because they weren't even convinced that atoms and molecules existed. But the link between heat and energy was crucial.

Beyond light

If you stand in bright sunlight, it's both light and warm. In 1800, the astronomer William Herschel explored which types of light are hottest. He used a prism to split light, and found that objects heated up most in light at the red end of the spectrum. Moving his thermometer beyond red, he discovered that infrared radiation—which seemed to be a kind of "invisible light"—is even hotter. A year after Herschel found infrared, Johann Ritter discovered ultraviolet at the opposite end of the visible spectrum. It turned out that both these, and visible light are all part of the electromagnetic spectrum. This was described by Scottish physicist James Clerk Maxwell.

ELECTROMAGNETIC SPECTRUM

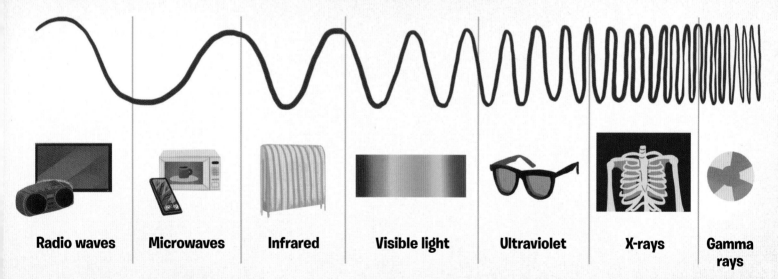

| Radio waves | Microwaves | Infrared | Visible light | Ultraviolet | X-rays | Gamma rays |

Making waves

Maxwell showed that electricity and magnetism are linked and that they produce waves of electromagnetic energy. In 1862, he found that waves of electromagnetic energy move at the speed of light—and so realized that visible light, infrared, and ultraviolet are part of the electromagnetic spectrum. Maxwell suspected that more types of energy would be discovered, and he was soon proved right.

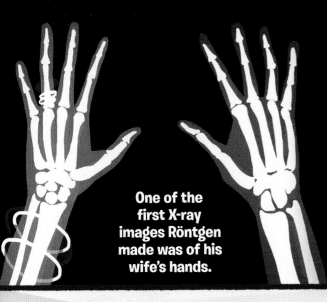

One of the first X-ray images Röntgen made was of his wife's hands.

Waves around the world

Heinrich Hertz discovered radio waves in 1888. These have a very long wavelength and were soon put to use carrying signals for communication systems. At first they were used to send telegrams; now they're used for everything from phones to television. In 1895, William Röntgen discovered X-rays, which have a short wavelength. They can pass through some materials but not others, including bone and metal. They're used to look inside things—anything from bodies to bags in an airport scanner.

Rays and particles

While investigating X-rays in France, Henri Becquerel found that uranium salts can be used to make an image on a photographic plate, just like X-rays. He had discovered radioactivity. Radioactivity now has many uses, from cancer treatments to nuclear power stations.

It soon emerged that not all radioactivity is the same. Ernest Rutherford, from New Zealand, found that some types of radiation can't go far through matter, while others can penetrate even thick metal. In total, Rutherford described three different types of radiation—alpha, beta, and gamma rays. In 1902, he showed that radioactivity happens as radioactive elements "decay": they lose energy and particles, changing from one element to another.

Marie Curie, a Polish chemist working in France, found several new radioactive elements and investigated the properties of radioactivity.

MAKING THE MODERN WORLD

The twentieth century saw scientists exploring the unseen—from the inside of atoms to the workings of the mind, from heredity to the energy locked within matter. It was a very different kind of study that placed a lot of confidence in the scientific method and in logic. While early experimenters worked mostly with results they could observe—the effects of gases, the twitching of muscles, and even the dividing of cells—the scientists of the twentieth century were, as often as not, working with the invisible. The role of mathematics in science grew more important as some topics could only be explored through equations. No one could look directly at atoms, or experiment with creating a universe, or try moving at the speed of light.

Investigating space
needed mathematics as
much as it needed
telescopes.

INTO THE ATOM

Since the ancient Greeks first suggested that matter is made of atoms, people had assumed that atoms are indivisible. Dalton realized that the atom of each chemical element is different, but did not suggest that atoms were made of parts. That discovery, and those that followed it, would change physics forever.

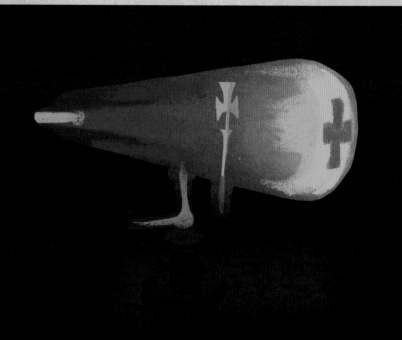

A Crooke's tube passes electrons through a vacuum toward a fluorescent coating, making a shadow where they are stopped by an object.

Taking atoms apart

The first component of atoms to be discovered was the electron, found in 1897 by J.J. Thomson. He had been experimenting with cathode rays, which are beams of energy that travel from the negative terminal in a circuit toward the positive terminal (anode). Johann Hittorf discovered cathode rays in 1869 when he showed that electricity passing through a vacuum, or near vacuum, in a glass tube could cast a shadow on a fluorescent surface. Ten years later, William Crookes showed that the "rays" are a stream of particles. Thomson worked out that the particles of the beam are only one thousandth the size of an atom, with a negative electrical charge. He showed that no matter what substance is used at the cathode, the rays are the same—electrons are identical, no matter what type of atom they come from.

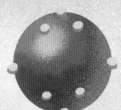

**Dalton's
solid sphere**

**Thomson's
plum pudding
model**

**Rutherford's early
model of a small nucleus
with randomly orbiting
electrons**

**Bohr's
planetary model**

Atom models

Dalton had thought of atoms as solid objects with no parts. Thomson showed that they contained electrons, and in 1904, he came up with a description of the atom that was like a pudding studded with currants—a blob of positively charged atom with electrons dotted through it. The same year, the Japanese physicist Hantaro Nagaoka suggested a planetary model of the atom. He put all the positive charge in a large central part (later named the nucleus), with the electrons moving randomly around it.

Ernest Rutherford, from New Zealand, accepted the idea of the positively charged tiny middle, though he initially didn't know that the electrons orbited. He worked with Niels Bohr on a new model, which they described in 1913. This had electrons orbiting in "shells"—imaginary spheres, one nested inside each other around the nucleus. Each shell could hold a set number of electrons.

Empty atoms

While Thomson had the electrons embedded in the positive part of the atom, Rutherford discovered that they are a very long way from it. In a famous experiment, he fired positively charged particles at gold foil. He found that some particles were sent off at a wide angle. This could only happen if they were repelled by, or bounced off, the positive nucleus of an atom. Because most did go straight through, most of the atom must be empty space, with just a small, dense nucleus. Later discoveries showed the nucleus is made of two types of particle: the positively charged proton (discovered in 1917) and the neutral neutron (discovered in 1933).

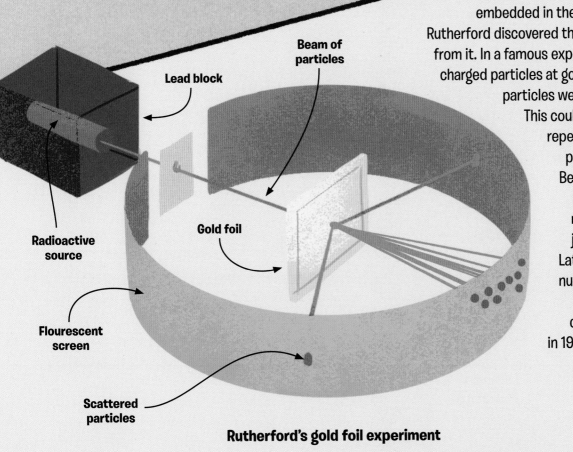

Lead block

Beam of
particles

Radioactive
source

Gold foil

Flourescent
screen

Scattered
particles

Rutherford's gold foil experiment

IT'S ALL RELATIVE

In the late 1800s, some people thought that all physics had been discovered and there was no more to do. Plunging into the structure of the atom showed that wasn't true. There was far more to discover, and it turned out to be stranger than anyone had imagined.

The end of physics?

In 1900, the German physicist Max Planck worked out that energy doesn't come in a constant stream, but in tiny packets, or "quanta." We now talk of "photons," the tiny packets of energy that make up light and other types of electromagnetic radiation. A photon has no mass—it's a little burst of energy that has a wavelength related to how much energy it has. Photons behave like both particles and waves depending on how we look at them.

The idea of quanta led to strange discoveries. One of those is that we can't know with certainty both the position and speed of a moving particle. Instead of certainty, physicists began to talk about probabilities—the probability that a particle was in a certain place. This led to another model of the atom, in which the nucleus is surrounded by a cloud of electrons that can't quite be pinned down.

In the quantum model of the atom described by Erwin Schrödinger in 1926, the electrons are more likely to be in some areas than others.

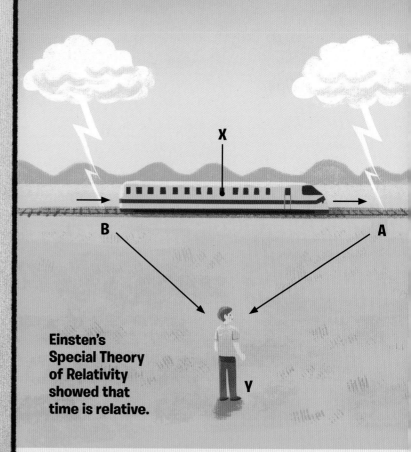

Einsten's Special Theory of Relativity showed that time is relative.

Einstein's ideas

Planck's quantum physics was soon followed by Albert Einstein's famous relativity theories: the theory of Special Relativity in 1905, and the theory of General Relativity in 1916. Einstein showed that some things we think of as unchanging, like how fast time passes, are relative—they change depending on circumstances.

Einstein explained that the speed of light is fixed, but how we experience time is relative. A person standing by a train track (**Y**) sees two simultaneous lightning strikes, one in front of a very fast train (**A**) and one behind it (**B**). A person in the middle of the train, though at **X**, would see the lightning in front factionally earlier. Because they're moving toward it, the light doesn't have as far to travel to them as the light from the flash behind, which they're moving away from. This shows that time is relative. To the person by the track, the events are simultaneous, but to the person on the train they're not.

86

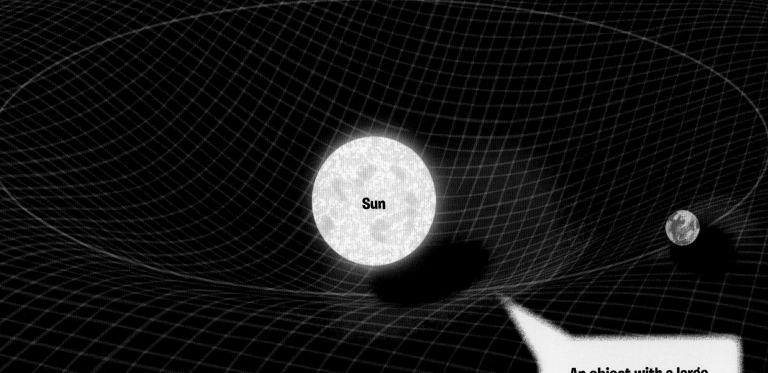

An object with a large mass bends spacetime more than an object with smaller mass, so the smaller object moves toward it.

Bending spacetime

Newton had explained gravity as a force acting between two objects that have mass. For example, the attraction between the Sun and planets keeps them in orbit. But in his General Theory of Relativity, Einstein saw gravity as a distortion of spacetime (the fabric of space and time). Spacetime dips around an object with a lot of mass, like the Sun. That means other objects will move toward it—rather like a small ball rolling toward a larger one on a blanket held taut.

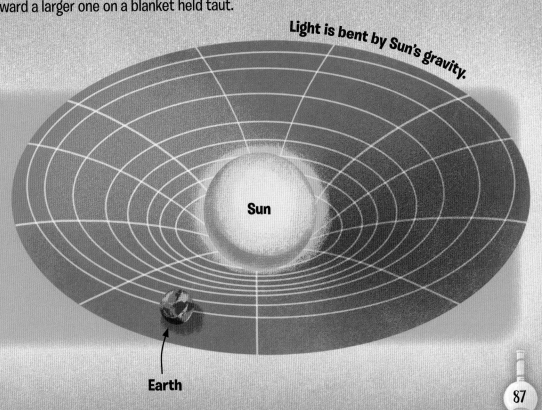

Light is bent by Sun's gravity.

Because spacetime is bent, even light is pulled toward objects with mass. His theory was shown to be correct in 1919 when measurements taken during an eclipse showed that light from a star was bent around the Sun.

Sun

Earth

INHERITING IDEAS

Mendel's work on how pea plants inherit traits had no immediate impact on science. But around 35 years later, it was rediscovered and people made the link between his findings and Darwin's theory of evolution. Finally, people began to understand how evolution might work.

From peas to flies

Before Mendel, people—including Darwin—believed that traits from two parents are blended when organisms reproduce. This meant that Mendel's purple and white pea plants should produce plants with pale mauve flowers—but they didn't. Trying to understand the mechanism of inherited traits, two biologists separately rediscovered Mendel's work in 1900, Hugo de Vries and Carl Correns. They realized that traits aren't generally blended but are inherited as whole units—white or purple, for instance.

An American biologist, Thomas Hunt Morgan, set to work to find out whether mutations (random changes in genes) could drive evolution. He worked with tiny fruit flies in a laboratory that become known as the "Fly Room."

Thomas Hunt Morgan

IN THE GENES

Each inherited trait is governed by a gene, which is part of a chromosome. Chromosomes are strands of genetic material, like a set of instructions for building an organism. The German scientist Walter Flemming first saw them in the nucleus of cells in 1882, but he didn't know what they did. Each chromosome is divided into areas, called genes, which each cover one aspect of the organism's inherited characteristics. An allele is a particular version of a gene. So, for example, a gene for wing shape could have alleles for normal or curved.

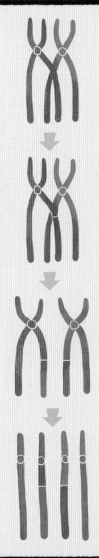

Genes

Chromosome

Crossing chromosomes

In 1911, Morgan noticed that some traits are often inherited together while others rarely are. He realized that the gene's position on the chromosome is fixed, and during meiosis, chromosomes might "cross over" and swap parts. If the genes for two traits lay close together on the chromosome, they could easily go together when this happened. His student Alfred Sturtevant worked out the order in which genes appeared on a chromosome, making the first gene map.

Crossing over of chromosomes means that the egg and sperm cells created in meiosis can contain blended chromosomes.

Fly experiments

Fruit flies live a short time and reproduce quickly and easily, making them a good choice for genetic experiments. Morgan soon bred flies with odd traits such as stunted wings. He studied the inheritance of red or white eyes, wing shape, and other traits.

Evolution and genes

Morgan originally thought that evolution couldn't work by collecting tiny inherited changes, but ended up saying that it did. In 1916, he stated that evolution happens because of mutations making inheritable changes that benefit organisms and are passed on from one generation to the next. Mutations take the form of changes to the genes on chromosomes. His work successfully drew together genetics and evolution, explaining what Darwin could not.

MOVING WORLD

The geologists of the nineteenth century had accepted that Earth is much older than the 6,000 years the Christian Church had previously claimed. They also agreed that Earth changes. The results of change were clear, from folded layers of rock to fossils of sea creatures found far inland. But they didn't know how those changes happened.

A good fit

For hundreds of years, people had noticed that if you remove the Atlantic Ocean from a map of the world, the coast of Africa fits neatly with the coast of South America—but no one could explain why. In 1912, the German weather-scientist Alfred Wegener shared his idea of "continental drift." He suggested that the continents slowly move around on the surface of Earth. South America had once been joined to Africa, but they'd drifted apart. Most geologists dismissed his idea immediately, partly because Wegener couldn't explain how the continents moved. But he had good evidence. He had examined rocks and fossils on both sides of the Atlantic and found that they matched. There are similar split bands of rock and fossils across other now-divided bands of land.

Africa

Lystrosaurus

Cynognathus

India

Glossopteris

South America

Antarctica

Australia

Fossils of *Cynognathus* and *Mesosaurus* are found in South America and West Africa; *Lystrosaurus* is found in Africa, India, and Antarctica; and the fern *Glossopteris* is found throughout the southern hemisphere.

Mesosaurus

Eurasia

North America

PANGEA

Africa

South America

India

Australia

Antarctica

All together

Wegener suggested that all the landmasses of Earth had once formed a single large continent, now called a supercontinent, which he named Pangea (meaning "all land"). This supercontinent broke apart over millions of years, as the continents drifted to their current positions. We now know that Pangea was only the last of several supercontinents that have formed and broken apart.

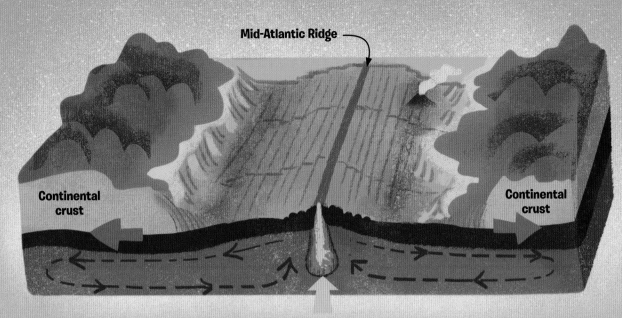

Mid-Atlantic Ridge

Continental crust

Continental crust

Magma

As magma bursts through the seabed and piles up, the existing rock is pulled and pushed toward the coast.

Stripy seabed

Excellent evidence for Wegener's idea emerged from scans of the seabed in the 1950s and 1960s. When ships began scanning the seabed with radar, scientists found a great ridge running along the Atlantic Ocean from north to south, like a seam of mountains. Earth's magnetic field, or polarity, reverses direction periodically, and the direction of its magnetism is sealed into the rocks.

Geologists found matching patterns of magnetic orientation on each side of the mid-ocean ridge.

This made it clear that the ocean grows from the middle, with new rock formed from magma (molten rock) rising from below the ocean floor, which can cause the landmasses to move. Scientists finally had a mechanism to explain continental drift.

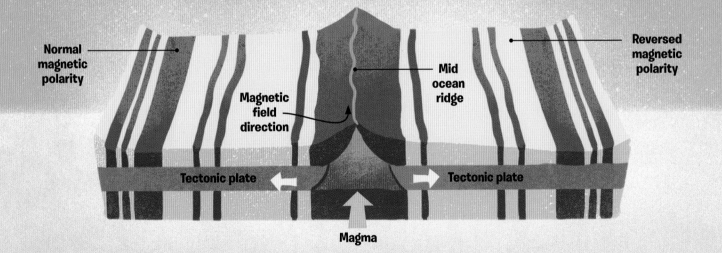

Normal magnetic polarity

Reversed magnetic polarity

Magnetic field direction

Mid ocean ridge

Tectonic plate

Tectonic plate

Magma

Broken plates

Wegener predicted that whatever moves the continents would be connected with other geological events, such as earthquakes, volcanic eruptions, and mountain-building. In 1967, it was all explained in terms of "tectonic plates"—vast slabs of Earth's surface, supported on a worldwide ocean of magma.

The plates are interlocking, but as they slowly move, they can collide, building mountains and volcanoes, and grate against each other, causing earthquakes. As plates under the ocean move, their edges dip under the continental land, melt back into Earth's crust, and feed volcanoes. They also push the continents around.

ENERGY FROM ATOMS

One of the results of Einstein's Special Theory of Relativity from 1905 was a very famous equation: $E=Mc^2$. This tells us that energy (E) and mass (M) are essentially interchangeable—they are the same thing. A tiny amount of mass (matter) can be converted into a huge amount of energy. This discovery is behind our understanding of how stars work, and lets us build power stations for nuclear energy. Both stars and power stations convert matter into energy.

Into the Sun

In 1925, the British astronomer Celia Payne discovered that the Sun is mostly made of hydrogen and helium, the two lightest gases in the Universe. At first, no one accepted her findings because people thought the Sun was made of the same materials as Earth. But in 1929, one of the men who had said she was wrong confirmed her result.

Celia Payne

Another English astronomer, Arthur Eddington, had already suggested in 1920 that the stars might be powered by the fusion (sticking together) of hydrogen atoms to make helium. Payne's discovery showed that this was possible. Atoms are forced together under immense pressure in the heart of a star so that they fuse. A little energy is released every time atoms are fused, producing the light, heat, and other radiation that pours from the Sun. The atoms that come together have very slightly more mass than the atoms that are made by fusion, with the extra mass escaping as energy and neutrons.

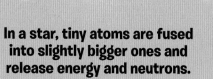

NUCLEAR FUSION

ENERGY

In a star, tiny atoms are fused into slightly bigger ones and release energy and neutrons.

NUCLEAR FISSION

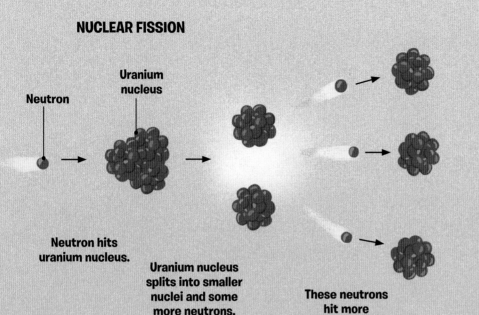

Neutron

Uranium nucleus

Neutron hits uranium nucleus.

Uranium nucleus splits into smaller nuclei and some more neutrons.

These neutrons hit more uranium nuclei.

Splitting the atom

Just as energy can be released when atoms are forced to stick together, so it can be released when atoms are broken apart. This is the basis of nuclear fission, used in nuclear power stations. Fission was first achieved by the Italian physicist Enrico Fermi in 1934.

Nuclear fission works by firing small particles at a large molecule to smash it apart. The smash releases energy, as well as more small neutrons moving at high speed. These particles can then collide with other molecules, making a "chain reaction."

Bombs and power stations

Research in nuclear fission was immediately directed toward making bombs during World War II. A group of scientists wrote to the American president encouraging the research, though some later regretted their support. They were afraid the Germans would develop a nuclear weapon first and win the war. In the end, America developed the atomic bomb and dropped two bombs on cities in Japan, causing devastation and killing many thousands of people.

Nuclear power station

Nuclear energy isn't only used for harm. The first nuclear reactor was built in 1942 and the first nuclear power station, using the energy from nuclear fission to generate electricity, opened in 1951 in Idaho, USA. Although nuclear power is a "clean" energy source because it doesn't produce carbon dioxide, several accidents at nuclear power stations have made many people wary of it.

BEYOND THE MILKY WAY

The night sky is full of stars, but there are also some bright fuzzy areas called "nebulae." Some of these were first listed by the French astronomer Charles Messier in 1774. As early as 1755, German philosopher Immanuel Kant suggested they might be other "universes"—which we would now call other galaxies. In the early 1900s, a lively debate began among astronomers. Some felt certain that the Milky Way is the whole Universe, but others thought there were galaxies beyond ours.

Modern telescopes such as the Hubble Space Telescope, named after Edwin Hubble, reveal distant galaxies in beautiful detail.

One or many?

In 1912, American astronomer Henrietta Levitt found a way of calculating the distance to pulsing stars called "cepheids." American astronomer Edwin Hubble found cepheids in spiral-shaped fuzzy patches, and showed in 1923 that they are so far away they are outside the Milky Way. The nebulae are, indeed, distant galaxies.

It started with a bang

A universe with other immense galaxies beyond our own is unimaginably large. Where could it have come from? In 1927, an answer was suggested by the Belgian astronomer Georges Lemaître, using a discovery made by Vesto Slipher. He had shown the wavelength of light from distant objects is stretched, showing they are moving away. Lemaître found that most stars are moving away, so the Universe is expanding (growing larger). That means it was previously smaller—much smaller. His idea, later called the "Big Bang," was that all space and time exploded into being long ago, starting as something incredibly small which he

The Universe began 13.8 billion years ago as an infinitely tiny point. Everything has evolved from it as it has spread to a huge size.

Jansky's radio antenna picked up radio signals from space.

Space radio

Evidence for the Big Bang had to wait for a new invention—the radio telescope. Optical telescopes work with light, but radio telescopes pick up a different part of the electromagnetic spectrum: radio waves. Karl Jansky accidentally discovered that space emits radio waves in 1932. He was investigating interference in radio equipment when he found a source of hissing which he later realized was coming from space. Now, radio telescopes are widely used to study radio waves from distant objects in space.

The shape of the solar system

Closer to home, our ideas of the solar system were updated. In 1930, American astronomer Clyde Tombaugh discovered the dwarf planet Pluto, beyond the orbit of Neptune. Its existence had been suggested already, because the orbits of Uranus and Neptune "wobble" in a way that could be explained by the gravity of another planet nearby. This gave Tombaugh a clue where to look.

Pluto

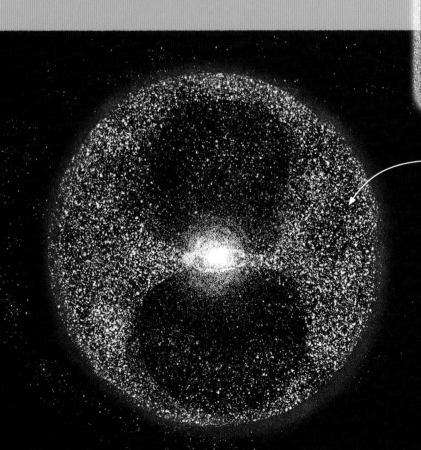

Oort Cloud

There is more to see beyond Pluto. In the 1950s, the Dutch astronomer Jan Oort predicted the existence of a vast, spherical cloud of objects made of rock and ice surrounding the solar system. The Oort Cloud, as it's now called, is the home to perhaps a trillion (million million) objects, including dust, rock, and comets.

BATTLING BACTERIA

In the 1860s, many people still believed that an imbalance of humors or "bad air" caused illness, but some scientists had begun to suspect that infections are caused by microscopic organisms. Work on cells soon led to the discovery of single-celled organisms called bacteria, some of which cause disease in humans or animals.

Nothing comes from nothing

In the 1850s, Remak and Virchow had shown that all cells in plants and animals come from other cells. The following decade, the French scientist Louis Pasteur showed that was true even of the tiniest organisms. He boiled broth in sealed flasks, then let air into some flasks and kept others sealed. The broth in flasks open to the air became cloudy as microbes grew in it. Pasteur had shown that spontaneous generation doesn't happen at all—even tiny microbes don't appear from nowhere. In the 1870s, he turned his attention to the role of microbes in disease.

Tiny agents of disease

Pasteur first investigated a disease in silkworms. He discovered that a certain type of bacteria, visible with his microscope, were always present in diseased animals but not healthy animals. He also found that some diseases are caused by something too small to see even with a microscope. These, we now know, are caused by viruses. While a bacterium is a cell, a virus is a chemical scrap, on the edge between living and non-living things. Viruses were first identified in the 1890s. Much smaller than bacteria, they couldn't be seen until the electron microscope was invented in the 1930s.

The idea that a single type of germ causes a single disease was set out by the German bacteriologist Robert Koch in 1884. His "germ theory" explained how to establish that a particular bacterium causes a particular disease.

Fighting back

Understanding the role of microbes helped to prevent disease. Simple handwashing in hospitals quickly reduced infections. From 1867, the Scottish surgeon Joseph Lister encouraged spraying the antiseptic carbolic acid during operations, making surgery safer. But what if infection had already taken hold?

In 1928, the Scottish microbiologist Alexander Fleming had been growing bacteria. He left his plates of bacteria in the sink and went away on a trip. On his return, he found that some of the bacteria had been killed by a fungus growing on the plates. The bacteria, called *Staphylococcus aurea*, cause illness in people, and so finding something that killed them was useful. Fleming called it penicillin. He couldn't extract penicillin from the fungus, though.

Nearly ten years later, Howard Florey and Ernst Chain set about making penicillin. They tried it on their first patient, who had an infected cut, in 1941. Although the patient improved at first, they ran out of penicillin before he could recover. But they had their answer, and the first antibiotic went into production in the USA. It saved the lives of thousands of soldiers in World War II.

Fleming's plate of penicillin

Alexander Fleming

INSIDE THE MIND

Psychology—the study of the mind—began only in the second half of the 1800s. Until the middle of the twentieth century, people knew little about how either normal or disordered minds work.

Ivan Pavlov

Drooling dogs

One of the most important early discoveries in psychology was accidental. In the 1890s, Ivan Pavlov was studying the production of saliva (spit) in dogs. He expected them to salivate when they tasted food. This is a natural reflex; dogs don't need to learn to do it. But they salivated as soon as they heard the footsteps of the assistant who fed them. This meant that dogs could be trained to associate a stimulus—such as the sound of a bell—with food. Their bodies would respond even before the food arrived. He called this "conditioning."

The "Little Albert" experiment showed that conditioning is important in human learning.

White rats and a crying baby

In 1920, two American psychologists investigated whether conditioning works in humans. John B. Watson and Rosalie Rayner conditioned a small child known as "Little Albert" to become afraid of white, furry objects. They let him pet a white rat, then made a loud, frightening sound. Albert soon began to cry at the appearance of the rat or anything similar—he had learned to associate it with fear. This unkind experiment would not be allowed today.

Mothering monkeys

As the twentieth century progressed, psychologists carried out more experiments on both humans and animals. Some were very cruel. Starting in 1958, the American psychology Harry Harlow investigated the relationship between mother monkeys and their infants by separating them at birth. He reared babies with two kinds of fake mother. One was made out of wire, and the other covered with soft fabric. Only the wire monkey provided food. Harlow found that babies went to the wire only to feed and then returned to the soft mother—comfort was more important than food. Monkeys reared entirely alone became seriously and permanently mentally unwell. He showed that infants need to form "attachments" to be emotionally and mentally healthy.

A baby monkey prefers a soft "mother" to one that provides food.

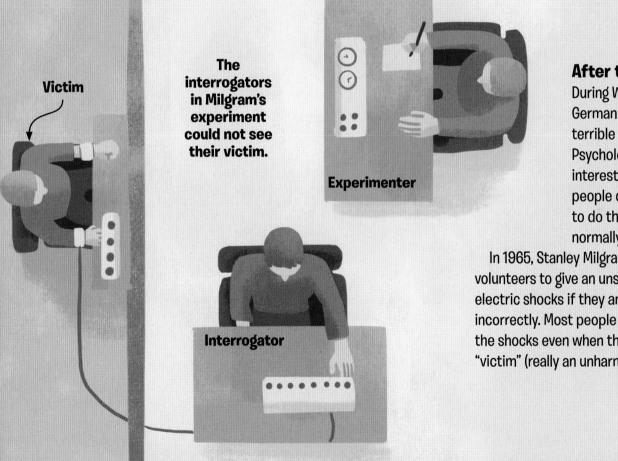

Victim

The interrogators in Milgram's experiment could not see their victim.

Experimenter

Interrogator

After the war

During World War II, the German Nazis committed terrible atrocities. Psychologists became interested in how ordinary people could be persuaded to do things they would normally consider wrong. In 1965, Stanley Milgram recruited volunteers to give an unseen victim electric shocks if they answered questions incorrectly. Most people continued to give the shocks even when they could hear the "victim" (really an unharmed actor) screaming.

Other experiments delivered similar findings. In 1971, Philip Zimbardo found that volunteers recruited to play the roles of "prison guards" soon began to treat "prisoners" very badly. In 1967, when Ron Jones' American high school students questioned his account of normal German people joining the Nazis, he set up a fake movement called the "Third Wave." Within days, his students were saluting, reporting rule-breakers, and keenly excluding "outsiders." He stopped the experiment early because they became too enthusiastic. People, it turns out, are more willing to do bad things than they think.

YOU ARE HERE

The pace of change in science ever since World War II has been phenomenal. Improvements in technology have made research possible that was unimaginable to earlier scientists. Much of today's work would be impossible without computers, as it would take entire lifetimes just to process the data collected. Computers aren't the only reason for such rapid progress. There are more people in the world now, and more of them are educated and able to work in scientific fields. Few women had such careers even 50 years ago, but now lots of women become respected experts in their chosen fields. Science has become global, too, with people training all over the world and working together on large, international projects.

UNLOCKING THE PAST

Finding that mutation drives evolution led people to think more about the organisms that had come and gone in the past. With the discovery of radioactivity, it became possible to put absolute dates on rocks and the fossils they contained. This work led to people wondering how and when life on Earth started.

Written in the rocks

One of the uses of radioactivity is dating ancient objects and rocks. A radioactive element slowly changes (decays) into another element. The time it takes for half of a sample to decay is its "half life," and can range from fractions of a second to billions of years. Scientists began to work out the age of rocks in 1904 and geologist Arthur Holmes perfected the method in 1911. He compared the amount of a radioactive element remaining in a rock with the amount of the products of its decay. The first rock Holmes dated came out at 370 million years old—far older than Earth was thought to be at the time! By 1921, the accepted age of Earth was 1.5 billion years. It's now thought to be 4.5 billion years old.

Dating rocks, dating life

Knowing the age of rocks enabled scientists to work out the age of fossils found in them. A much older Earth meant more time for life to emerge and evolution to work.

For a long time, the earliest known fossils were from the Cambrian period, 539–485 million years ago. These were soft-bodied organisms found in the Burgess Shale in Canada in 1909. Soft bodies don't fossilize as well as bones, teeth, and shells (which all evolved later), so there seemed little hope of finding earlier fossils. Then in 1957 an English schoolboy, Roger Mason, found a fossil that was 550–570 million years old.

Charnia **was a strange organism that lived on the seabed 550 million years ago.**

The strange organisms fossilized in the Burgess Shale, discovered in 1909, lived over 500 million years ago. They were not properly studied until 1962.

The start of life

Pasteur had shown that life doesn't come from non-living matter, yet that's exactly how the first life must have appeared. Scientists believe it must have happened in stages, with chemicals essential to life appearing first. In the 1920s, Alexander Oparin and J.B.S. Haldane suggested that organic molecules formed in a hot chemical "soup" on early Earth. This was tested by Stanley Miller in 1953. He mixed chemicals thought to be in Earth's early atmosphere and used electrical sparks to mimic lightning strikes. Several organic chemicals important to life formed in his flask.

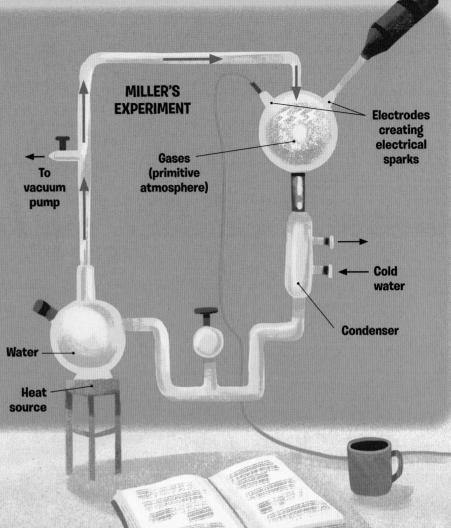

MILLER'S EXPERIMENT

Electrodes creating electrical sparks

Gases (primitive atmosphere)

To vacuum pump

Cold water

Condenser

Water

Heat source

Archaea can live in volcanic pools. Perhaps they did so 3–4 billion years ago.

Hostile planet

Darwin suggested in 1871 that life might have started in a warm pool, which sounds pleasant. But it might not have been so nice. A new class of microorganisms called archaea were found in the 1970s in the volcanic pools of Yellowstone Park, USA, and showed that life could survive in very hostile environments. Archaea live everywhere, even in water that is scalding hot, acidic, or full of dissolved chemicals such as salt. Where life began is still an open question.

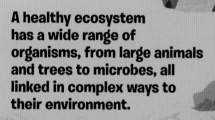

A healthy ecosystem has a wide range of organisms, from large animals and trees to microbes, all linked in complex ways to their environment.

CONNECTED LIVES

Until 1935, people tended to study plants and animals in isolation. That year, British ecologist Arthur Tansley first talked about "ecosystems"—entire systems consisting of an environment with its climate, land structure, soil chemistry, habitats, and all its living things. The idea of ecosystems proved to be very important in understanding how humans change the environment, and the far-reaching impact this can have.

Messing things up

In the late 1800s, many countries struggled to grow enough food to feed their populations. After discovering that plants grow better when given fertilizer containing the chemical nitrogen, chemists rushed to find a way of making nitrogen-rich fertilizer. Fritz Haber discovered the solution in 1909, with a process that takes nitrogen from the air and "fixes" it in a form that plants can absorb from the soil. Soon, farming depended heavily on fertilizer. Other chemical aids soon arrived, including pesticides to kill insects that harm crops, and weedkillers to remove unwanted plants. At the same time, industrial processes made more waste that poured into rivers and the air, becoming pollution. The twentieth century saw serious environmental problems caused by human activity.

Spraying DDT on fields of crops led to the death of useful insects, birds, mammals, and fish as well as troublesome insects.

Unintended victims

During World War II, the insecticide DDT was used to kill lice, fleas, and insects that carried diseases between people. After the war, farmers began spraying it on crops to protect them from destructive insects. DDT built up in the soil and passed through food chains, soon affecting animals that ate insects, and the animals that ate those insects. Fish living in rivers contaminated with DDT also died. The biologist Rachel Carson brought the catastrophic impact of DDT to public attention in 1962. The people using, making, and promoting DDT tried to discredit her work, but eventually the chemical was banned for agricultural use in many places. It was the first time that the impact of a chemical on ecosystems had been revealed as highly damaging. Carson's work triggered the environmental movement of the 1960s, in which people began to think about the need to protect the environment.

Rachel Carson

A living planet?

In 1974, the British scientist James Lovelock went further than most people who are interested in the natural environment. He suggested that Earth is, or works like, a huge living organism. His theory, called Gaia theory, explains the planet as a self-healing and self-regulating system in which all aspects—climate, chemistry, landscape, and living organisms—are closely connected and work together. Humans disrupt this system by producing too much pollution, killing organisms, destroying their environments, and interfering in other ways with the natural balance of the living world. These ideas are now accepted in mainstream science, even though his idea of Earth as a living organism is not.

JUMBLING GENES

Morgan's work on fruit flies revealed that chromosomes pass inherited traits between parent and child, but no one knew exactly how. In 1944, scientists discovered that DNA, the chemical that makes chromosomes, carries the genetic instructions for making an organism.

Dolly the sheep was a clone —an exact genetic copy of her mother, with identical DNA—produced in 1996.

HOW IT WORKS

A DNA molecule looks like a ladder that has been twisted into a helix (spiral). Each "rung" is made of two "bases." These always form the same pairs—adenine (A) with thymine (T) and cytosine (C) with guanine (G). A gene is a sequence of rungs. Genes differ in how the pairs of bases are arranged. There are four possible arrangements for each pair—AT, TA, CG, GC. Just 10 pairs give more than a million possibilities. Many genes have thousands of pairs, so there's plenty of scope for difference.

From molecule to human

Your own DNA (deoxyribonucleic acid) holds a "code" for building you as an individual and running your body. It's present in nearly every cell. Your DNA is unique—unless you have an identical twin, when your DNA will be very similar to theirs. How this code works was revealed after three chemists, Rosalind Franklin, James Watson, and Francis Crick, worked out the structure of the DNA molecule in 1953.

Working with genes

Genome "sequencing" involves listing all the base pairs on all of an organism's chromosomes, in order. The first genome sequenced, in 1976, belonged to a virus. The massive task of mapping the whole human genome took 13 years, from 1990 to 2003. There are more than three billion bases on the 23 human chromosomes. But knowing the sequence still doesn't tell scientists what each gene does. That's a slow process of discovery, seeing how differences between organisms line up with differences in their DNA.

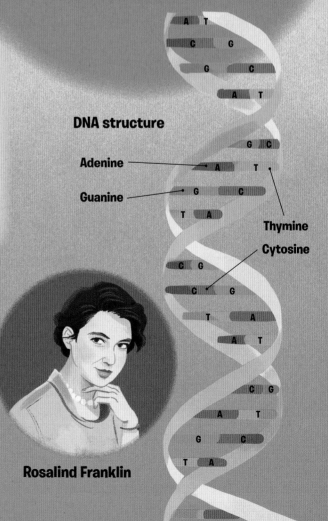

DNA structure

Adenine

Guanine

Thymine

Cytosine

Rosalind Franklin

Genes working for us

The first work with genes began in 1972, when scientists developed a way of sticking bits of DNA together. One of the earliest uses, in 1978, was making insulin. Our bodies usually produce insulin, but people with diabetes can't make it and need to inject it to stay healthy. Insulin is now made in huge vats by genetically changed bacteria. The human gene for making insulin is put into bacteria, then the bacteria are grown. They produce the insulin, and we harvest it.

Using bacteria to produce insulin

Recombinant bacterium

Fermentation tank

Recombinant bacterium produces insulin

Insulin is harvested

Gene editing (changing genes) has many uses. It can make crops that are resistant to disease or pests, or that contain extra nutrients. It can make unusual pets or animals to use in science, such as glow-in-the dark mice or day-glo fish. Scientists take the genes for the wanted trait and add them to a cell that will grow into a new organism.

Talking point

Gene editing could fix genetic conditions that harm people, and recreate extinct animals. These possibilities are controversial. Should we be doing things like this? People disagree about what should be allowed.

Golden rice (left) is genetically modified to be more nutritious than white rice. Development started in 1982 and it was first grown in 2004.

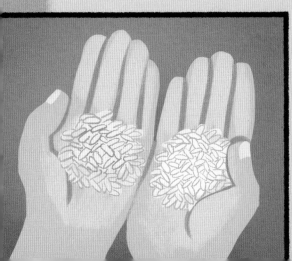

The last thylacine died in 1936 in an Australian zoo. In 2022, a project began to recreate the thylacine and reintroduce it to Tasmania.

OUT OF THIS WORLD

The radio telescope changed astronomy for ever, and later in the century, so did space travel. Visiting places in space has revealed more than we can learn about the solar system from Earth. But distances in space are vast, and space travel can't replace the function of telescopes. Some of the best tools for studying the distant Universe are sited in space.

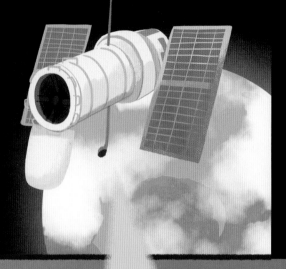

The Hubble Space Telescope was launched in 1990. Telescopes in space bypass interference from Earth's atmosphere.

Blast off!

Modern rockets were developed as weapons in World War II, but used for space exploration soon after. Both the USSR (now Russia) and USA sent rockets into space from the 1940s. Some carried animals to test whether space travel was safe for living things. The USSR took the next steps, putting a small satellite into orbit in 1957 and the first astronaut in space in 1961. The USA put humans on the Moon in 1969. Uncrewed spacecraft (without humans on board) have visited other planets and even ventured beyond the solar system.

Decades of rocket science lay behind Apollo 11's success in taking astronauts to the Moon.

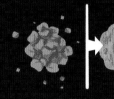

Early Earth and its Moon

Earth isn't alone in space—it has a Moon. There have been several theories about how the Moon formed. Currently, many scientists accept an idea suggested in 1946 and revived in 1969—that another planet (now named "Theia") crashed into Earth, and the Moon formed from a molten mix of both. The chemical composition of Moon rock supports this idea.

Making planets

Rock from the Moon, meteorites, and rock on other planets and asteroids all tell us about the materials in the early solar system that made Earth. Scientists had little idea how Earth formed until recently. In 1969, the Russian cosmologist Victor Safronov suggested the solar system started as a disk of gas and dust whirling around the forming Sun. Specks of matter collided and stuck together, growing larger. As they grew, their gravity increased, so they pulled in more matter. The pressure of rock pushing together heated the baby planet until it melted in the middle. The middle of Earth is still very hot, 4.5 billion years later.

The first rover on Mars, Sojourner, landed in 1997. Examination of the surface of Mars tells us about the early solar system.

Major mysteries

In the 1930s, the astronomer Fritz Zwicky calculated that some clusters of galaxies contain much more mass than we can see. Thirty years later, it appeared that this is true of individual galaxies, too. By 1980, it was clear that about a quarter of the Universe is mysterious "dark matter." Things got even stranger. Measurements in 1998 showed that the Universe is expanding faster and faster. "Dark energy" seems to be pushing matter apart. Dark energy makes up 70 percent of the Universe—leaving only about 5 percent for all the normal, non-dark matter.

FAR, FAR AWAY

In 1995, astronomers found the first proof of an exoplanet—a planet outside our solar system. Since then, thousands more have been discovered. There could be billions in the galaxy. This raises the question of whether there are living things on any other planets. Scientists are looking for past or present microbes on Mars, and for signs hinting at life on exoplanets.

Exoplanets are too far away to see, but astronomers can find out a little about what they are made of and how hot they are.

RAYS IN ACTION

The discovery of the full electromagnetic spectrum, from radio waves to gamma rays, gave scientists new tools to work with. X-rays were immediately used in medicine. Radio waves have been used more and more for communications. The first microwave cooker was invented in 1945. But as well as directing electromagnetic radiation to work for us, we've been gathering it from space to learn about the Universe.

We use rays like radiowaves and microwaves every day without thinking about it.

Energy and waviness

The various types of electromagnetic radiation are all rays of energy with different wavelengths. Science uses them in several ways. We can exploit their "waviness" by using them to bounce off things and be reflected back, using them to cast shadows, or coding information into the size of the waves. Or we can exploit their energy—such as using the energy of microwaves to heat up food, or concentrating light into a laser beam to cut through things.

Bouncing waves

In 1937, weather researcher Robert Watson-Watt outlined a system for spotting thunderstorms by sending radio signals into the air and tracking how they were reflected back. This became radar, soon used to spot planes as well as weather systems.

Radar works by sending out radio waves that bounce off a plane or other object. The receiver picks up the reflected waves.

Sonar and ultrasound both use sound waves (which are not electromagnetic) in the same way as radar uses radiowaves. Ultrasound is used in medicine and undersea exploration. In World War II, ultrasound was used to spot submarines. After the war, ultrasound investigation of the seabed revealed the mid-ocean ridges that confirmed Wegener's theory of continental drift.

In 1958, ultrasound was first used in medicine. Sound waves pass through the body harmlessly—they are safer than X-rays. The ultrasound machine can draw a picture of things inside the body from the echo that comes back.

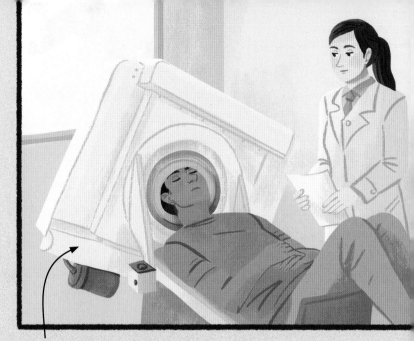

A CT (computer-aided tomography) scan takes multiple X-ray images.

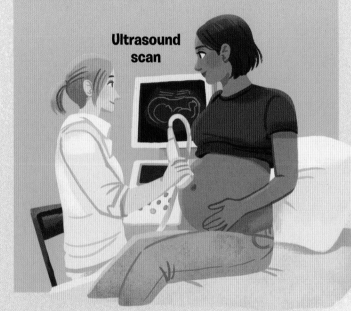

Ultrasound scan

Shadow waves

Medical X-rays work differently to ultrasounds. X-rays are stopped by dense matter, such as bone, and produce a shadow on a plate behind, as Röntgen discovered. From the 1970s, a new type of X-ray scan took images of "slices" through the body and built them into a 3D image, called a CT scan.

Information from waves

A radio telescope scans the sky for radio waves coming from distant objects, just like an optical telescope collects light from distant objects. Objects in space produce other types of radiation, too. There have been X-ray telescopes since 1962, and microwave telescopes since 1989. One of the most important discoveries was cosmic microwave background radiation (CMBR). This is the radiation left over from the Big Bang. It was first predicted in 1948, but discovered accidentally in 1964. Two engineers working on a radio receiver found a persistent type of interference that they couldn't get rid of. It turned out to be the CMBR—evidence of the Big Bang. Scientists studying the CMBR using microwave telescopes soon found that it isn't evenly spread through the Universe. Its "lumpiness"—uneven temperature—reveals where galaxies and stars would later form.

The CMBR map shows hotter and colder areas of the Universe 380,000 years ago. Galaxies would form in the hotter areas. The first map like this was made in 1982.

NEW KINDS OF MIND

Science often builds on ideas and discoveries that have come before, as our understanding grows over time. There are sometimes big surprises, particularly in astronomy, when new inventions uncover things that were previously hidden—but on Earth, big changes are rare. Yet that's just what happened in the second half of the twentieth century, when botanists discovered that plants communicate with each other in ways no one had suspected. They are far more resourceful and cooperative than we ever imagined.

Keeping in touch

In the 1920s, scientists discovered that ethylene gas can make fruit ripen. All ripe fruit produces ethylene, which also triggers ripening. This helps plants by getting all their fruit to ripen at the same time. A plant relies on animals eating its fruit to spread seeds, so if fruit ripens together, that will attract animals to come and eat it. But this is just a tiny part of how plants use chemicals as signals.

One tomato plant will warn a nearby plant if it's attacked by insects.

A study in the 1980s found that when trees were attacked by caterpillars, they produced a chemical that floated through the air, "warning" other plants. When a tree detected the warning, it produced a chemical in its own leaves that made them unattractive to the caterpillars. In 2011, scientists found that pea plants send a chemical signal when stressed by drought (lack of water). When other plants nearby pick up the signal, they prepare by closing their stomata (the holes in their leaves, through which they lose water).

Some plants go even further. A study in 1995 found that some plants, when attacked by insects, produce a chemical to attract predators that will attack the insects.

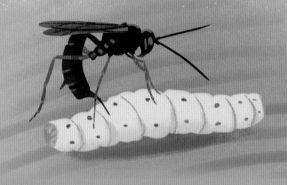

Maize plants attract parasitic wasps that lay their eggs inside the Egyptian cotton leaf worm.

A "wood-wide" web

Suzanne Simard made one of the most astonishing discoveries about plant communication in 1997. She discovered that a huge network of underground fungus links the roots of trees and other plants and carries chemical signals between them.

This "mycorrhizal" network enables trees to share nutrients when some are struggling, or to support young trees. It enables a dying tree to donate its useful nutrients to others. Some plants help others they are related to, more than they will help "strangers." Scientists are only just beginning to explore how plants use this network. They estimate that the total fungal network worldwide, in just the top 10 cm (4 in) of soil, is long enough to stretch halfway across the galaxy!

Hub or "mother" trees are the most inter-connected in a forest. They play an important role in the flow of resources. These trees supply nutrients to young trees—especially those they are related to—and even change their own root structure to make room for them.

IN THE GREENHOUSE

One of the biggest stories in modern science is climate change: why it is happening, what it will mean, and what we can do about it. It concerns scientists of all types, including chemists, physicists, biologists, meteorologists, engineers, and ecologists.

Not the first

Humans are not the first organism to have changed the climate. Bands of red, rust-stained rock from 2.4 billion years ago, noticed by scientists in the 1970s, are evidence of the first appearance of oxygen in Earth's sea and air.

The oxygen was probably produced by the first photosynthesizing microorganisms that took in carbon dioxide and released oxygen. This period, called the Great Oxygenation Event, was followed by a period of such severe cold that the entire Earth was frozen for hundreds of millions of years. Another, less extreme, global freeze was probably caused by the first trees releasing more oxygen and reducing the level of carbon dioxide 360 million years ago.

We're now doing the reverse—warming Earth by releasing a lot of carbon dioxide quickly.

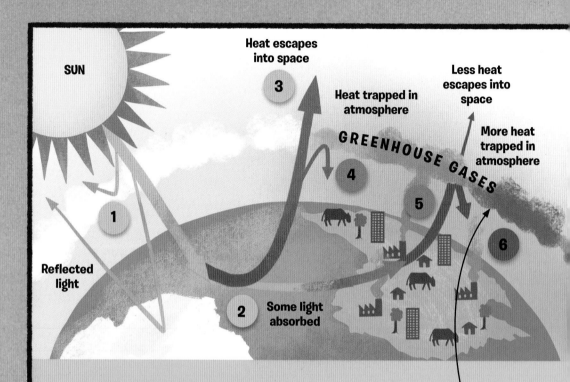

A layer of "greenhouse gases" that reflects heat back to Earth, rather than allowing it to escape into space, causes the planet to warm up.

Early warnings

In 1824, the French physicist Joseph Fourier realized that the atmosphere traps heat near Earth's surface. In 1861, an Irish physicist, John Tyndall, found that some gases, including water vapor, act like a "blanket" that keeps heat close to Earth's surface. And in 1896, the Swedish chemist Svante Arrhenius pointed out that burning fossil fuels such as gas and coal would increase the "greenhouse effect" that Tyndall had identified.

Arrhenius calculated that doubling the amount of carbon dioxide in the atmosphere would raise the temperature on Earth by a few degrees Celsius. In 1938, engineer Guy Callendar showed that the concentration of carbon dioxide and the global temperature had both risen over the last 100 years. By 1957, scientists knew that the extra carbon dioxide being produced would build up. By 1965, scientists advised that climate change was a very real concern.

On the way up

Scientists have monitored the amount of carbon dioxide in the atmosphere constantly since 1958. It keeps going up, but there is a peak-and-trough pattern within each year. This reflects the higher use of fossil fuels during winter in the northern hemisphere (where most people live).

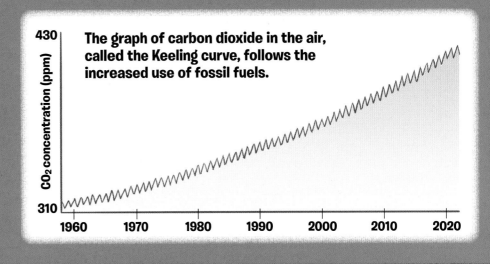

The graph of carbon dioxide in the air, called the Keeling curve, follows the increased use of fossil fuels.

Water is darker than ice and absorbs more heat. Melting ice produces a feedback effect of more heating and more melting.

Predicting the future

Scientists first used computer models to predict the outcomes of climate change in 1967. They calculated that doubling the level of carbon dioxide would raise the temperature by 2.4°C (6.8°F). In 1988, James Hansen announced that global heating was already happening. Predictions for the impact of higher temperatures include more severe weather events, such as heatwaves, droughts, floods, and hurricanes, and rising sea levels. As ice melts near the poles and high up on mountains, meltwater will flow into the sea, and flood low-lying islands and coastal areas.

A rise in global temperatures will lead to more severe droughts, wildfires, storms, and floods.

CHALLENGES FOR SCIENCE

Throughout human history, science has explained the world around us and helped us to solve problems. It has improved our lives in many ways. Now, some immense challenges face us. We hope that science will help us find the way forward. But science faces challenges of its own, too.

Practical help

There are many practical problems we want science to help us solve, including climate change, the need for "clean" energy, and a solution to falling biodiversity (the variety of living things). We hope for new medical treatments, sustainable food supplies, and answers to questions about the nature of the Universe.

Science has revealed the diversity of life on Earth, as well as the damage we are doing to it. Can it help us stop and repair that damage?

Science can help solve problems like our reliance on fossil fuels for energy.

Informed consent

We're on the brink of being able to do some very powerful things with science. We can edit genes to change organisms, including humans. We can make computers with reasoning power comparable to our own. We can make microscopic machinery (nanotechnology) that we might release into our bodies or the environment. As a society, we must decide how these things will be used, and what we will tolerate. Scientists need to help us make choices that are as informed as possible.

For better or worse

Science itself is neither good nor bad—it is a process of discovery. But what people do with the findings of science can be good or bad. We can make poisons or medicines; bombs or power supplies. There can be unintended or unforeseen consequences. When Albert Einstein discovered that energy and matter are interchangeable, he didn't anticipate the atomic bombs it makes possible. When people made DDT to kill lice, they didn't realize it would destroy whole ecosystems. The science that has helped us make our modern lives has also given us the problem of dealing with the waste and pollution it produces and the risk of running out of the resources it relies on. One of the challenges for science is to foresee and avoid future problems.

We need to deal with the waste that our modern lives produce, finding ways to extract valuable resources from it and keep the world clean.

Some people didn't believe covid was real, or refused vaccines.

Anti-science

Since the late twentieth century, some people have begun to distrust scientists and science. They suspect that scientists work with big businesses or governments to deceive us, or can't be trusted now because they have made mistakes in the past. During the covid-19 pandemic, some people didn't believe that covid was real, or thought that it had been manufactured and released on purpose, or worried that vaccines had been engineered to harm them. Online misinformation makes it easy for people to find alternative, unreliable accounts of scientific subjects.

It's hard to see how science can face the challenge of public distrust, except through education. Knowing about science helps you to understand it. Learning to assess information and know which sources to trust will help you deal confidently with scientific ideas. Scientists, too, must remain open to criticism and own up to mistakes when they make them.

SCIENCE OF THE FUTURE

What will science bring us in the future? There could always be surprises in store, but some of the problems that scientists are working on now are likely to bear fruit in the coming decades.

Air travel uses a great deal of energy. Hydrogen-powered planes are in development to allow "clean" flying.

Energy for all

One of the biggest problems in the world today is finding sources of energy that don't contribute to climate change. "Green" or "clean" energy must replace fossil fuels, to reduce the damage our energy use does to the planet. The target of "net zero"—producing no extra carbon dioxide—is still a long way off. Solar, wind, wave, nuclear, and geothermal power are all options we already have. Other possibilities are still being explored. Hydrogen as a source of energy produces only water as waste. Nuclear fusion—making energy in the same way as stars, by fusing atoms together—is still some way off, but scientists are making progress. A breakthrough in 2022 offers hope that it might become possible by firing a powerful laser at a capsule containing hydrogen. The heat and pressure force the hydrogen atoms to fuse and make helium, releasing energy as they do so.

Materials for all

Our modern lives use a lot of resources. But many of these are running out, from fossil fuels to rare metals used in electronics. As well as perfecting ways of recycling and recovering as many materials as possible, science is exploring more outlandish solutions, including mining asteroids in space for metals we need.

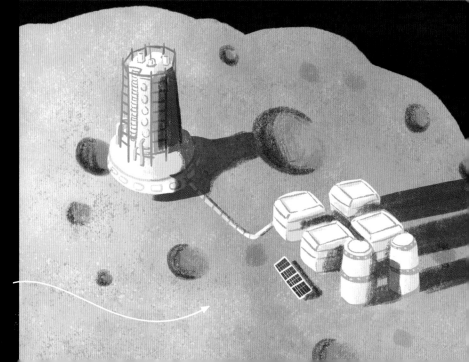

Asteroids are made of the same materials as our planet, so harvesting minerals and metals from them could provide resources we need.

The inside of a 3D-printed bone is spongy, just like the inside of a real bone.

Medicine for all

Advances in medicine happen all the time. The covid-19 pandemic led to the rapid development of new vaccines, including mRNA vaccines that don't use any of the original disease-causing agent.

There are plenty of challenges in medicine for science to address. Microbes have become resistant to our antibiotics, making infections harder to treat—so we need to find and develop new treatments. Although we can often replace faulty body parts with new ones in transplant operations, there are never as many organs available as patients need. Medical scientists are working on growing human-compatible organs in other animals, making artificial organs, and even growing organs from human tissue on an artificial framework. All of these methods could provide organs for people who need them without having to wait for a natural organ donation. Some structures, such as bone, can even be created by 3-D printing. Fake skin for transplants and blood for transfusions are also being explored.

Personalized medicine, which targets a treatment to each patient's genetic make-up, is another advance on the horizon. In 2023, a deadly genetic condition was reversed in a baby by gene editing. Genetic material was taken from the baby, fixed, and returned to her bones so that the future cells produced would be healthy.

Science still has a great deal to offer—it just needs future scientists with vision, compassion, and imagination. Could that be you?

Around 1.7 million years ago

Early humans shaped stones into hand axes.

12,000 years ago (10,000 BCE)

As farming began, people bred from the plants and animals that had the features they preferred, slowly changing their crops and livestock.

1.5–0.8 million years ago

People began using fire for heat, light, to scare away animals, and to change materials.

4500–4000 BCE

Nabta Playa in Egypt was arranged as a calendar, tracking the Sun.

3000 BCE

Sumerian astronomers recorded observations of the night sky on clay tablets.

35,000 years ago

People made and used pigments to paint pictures, carefully observing and depicting the animals around them.

Burning ores to release molten metal enabled people to make more precise shapes and useful tools. Later (4500 BCE), they mixed tin into liquid copper to make bronze.

5500 BCE

Eratosthenes calculated the circumference of Earth.

Arab astronomers developed instruments and techniques to make advances in observing the stars and planets.

832 CE

The House of Wisdom in Baghdad collected scientific works and translated them into Arabic. Arab scientists then built on this knowledge.

400 BCE

Hippocrates described health in terms of the balance of the bodily "humors."

Alchemists in China discovered how to make gunpowder. They used it for the first rockets, making fireworks and weapons.

850

Second century CE

The Greek model of a geocentric solar system, originally developed around 400 BCE, was perfected by Ptolemy and lasted 1,500 years.

Eleventh century

Shen Kuo worked out that Earth's climate has changed over very long periods.

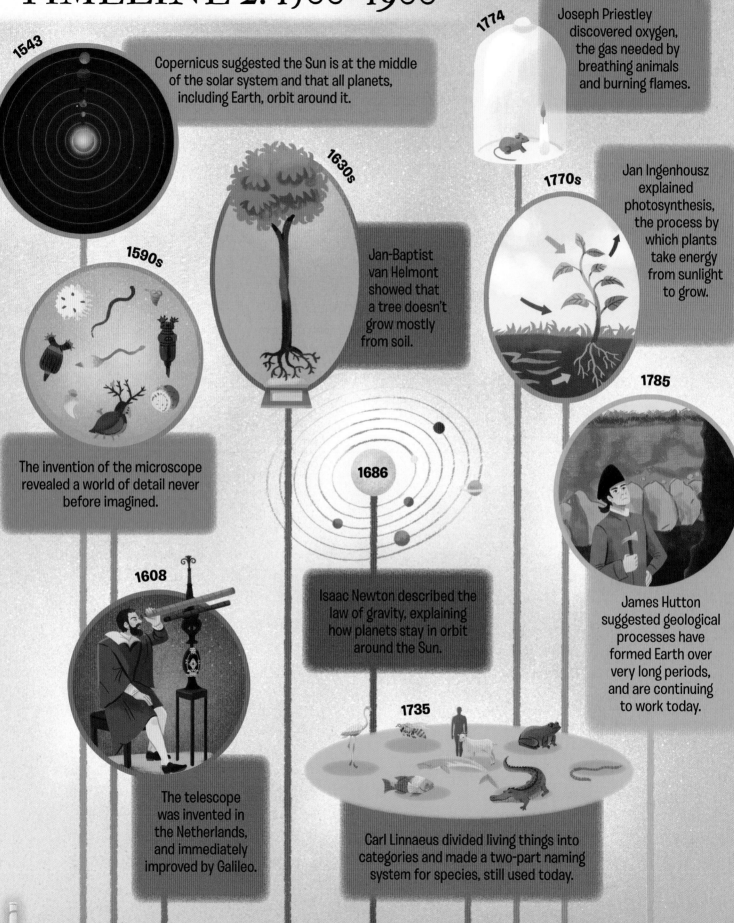

TIMELINE 2: 1500–1900

1543 Copernicus suggested the Sun is at the middle of the solar system and that all planets, including Earth, orbit around it.

1774 Joseph Priestley discovered oxygen, the gas needed by breathing animals and burning flames.

1630s Jan-Baptist van Helmont showed that a tree doesn't grow mostly from soil.

1770s Jan Ingenhousz explained photosynthesis, the process by which plants take energy from sunlight to grow.

1590s The invention of the microscope revealed a world of detail never before imagined.

1785 James Hutton suggested geological processes have formed Earth over very long periods, and are continuing to work today.

1686 Isaac Newton described the law of gravity, explaining how planets stay in orbit around the Sun.

1608 The telescope was invented in the Netherlands, and immediately improved by Galileo.

1735 Carl Linnaeus divided living things into categories and made a two-part naming system for species, still used today.

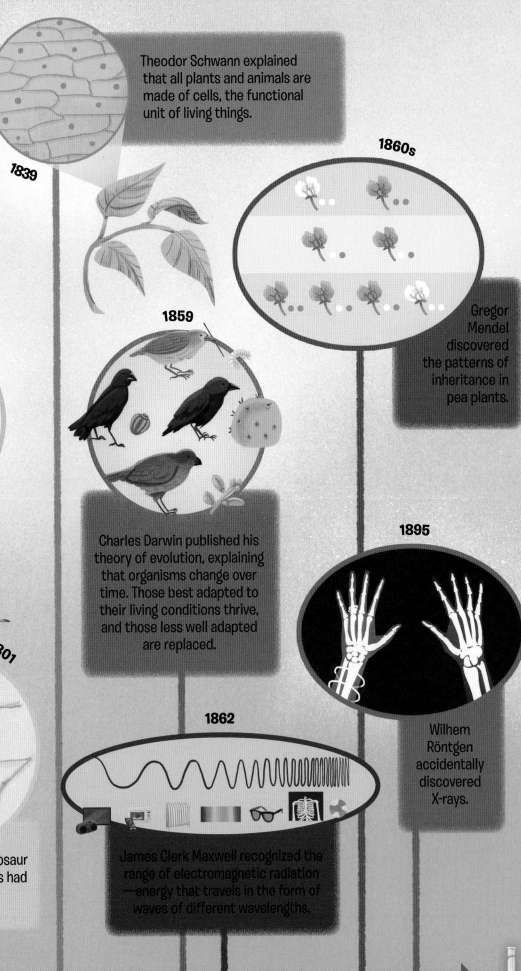

Luigi Galvani showed that electricity makes muscles contract, enabling movement.

1791

Theodor Schwann explained that all plants and animals are made of cells, the functional unit of living things.

1839

1860s

Gregor Mendel discovered the patterns of inheritance in pea plants.

1800

1859

John Dalton explained that each of the chemical elements has its own unique type of atom.

1801

Charles Darwin published his theory of evolution, explaining that organisms change over time. Those best adapted to their living conditions thrive, and those less well adapted are replaced.

1895

Wilhem Röntgen accidentally discovered X-rays.

Cosimo Collini discovered a pterosaur fossil, firm evidence that animals had gone extinct in the past.

1862

James Clerk Maxwell recognized the range of electromagnetic radiation —energy that travels in the form of waves of different wavelengths.

1791 1800 1801   1839   1859 1862   1860s 1895 1900

TIMELINE 3: 1900–NOW

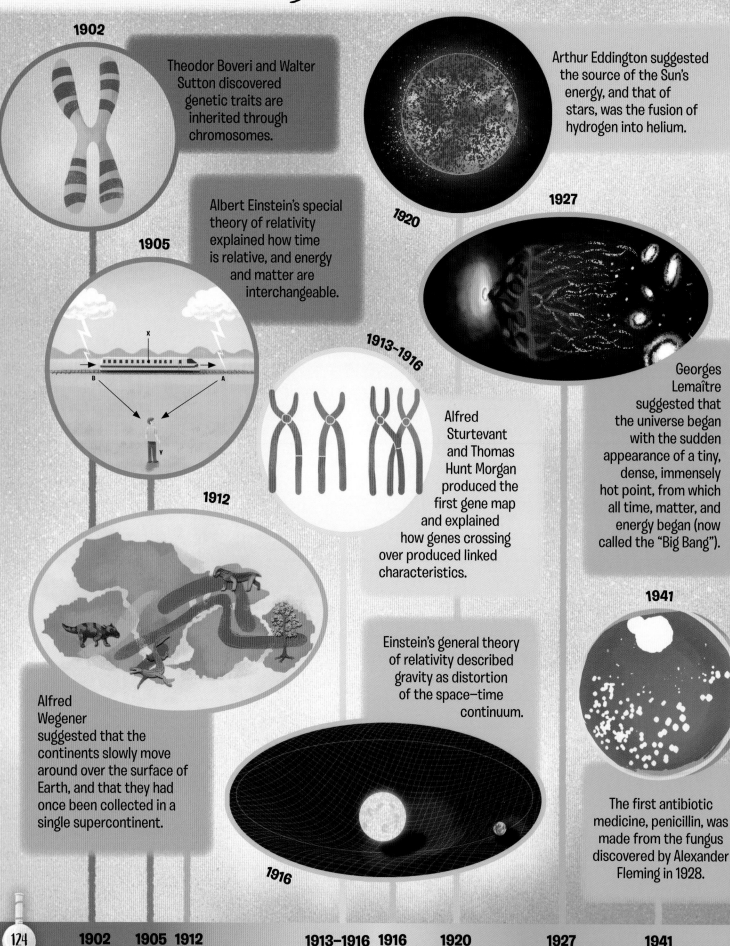

1902
Theodor Boveri and Walter Sutton discovered genetic traits are inherited through chromosomes.

Arthur Eddington suggested the source of the Sun's energy, and that of stars, was the fusion of hydrogen into helium.

1920

1905
Albert Einstein's special theory of relativity explained how time is relative, and energy and matter are interchangeable.

1927

1913–1916
Alfred Sturtevant and Thomas Hunt Morgan produced the first gene map and explained how genes crossing over produced linked characteristics.

Georges Lemaître suggested that the universe began with the sudden appearance of a tiny, dense, immensely hot point, from which all time, matter, and energy began (now called the "Big Bang").

1912
Alfred Wegener suggested that the continents slowly move around over the surface of Earth, and that they had once been collected in a single supercontinent.

Einstein's general theory of relativity described gravity as distortion of the space–time continuum.

1941
The first antibiotic medicine, penicillin, was made from the fungus discovered by Alexander Fleming in 1928.

1916

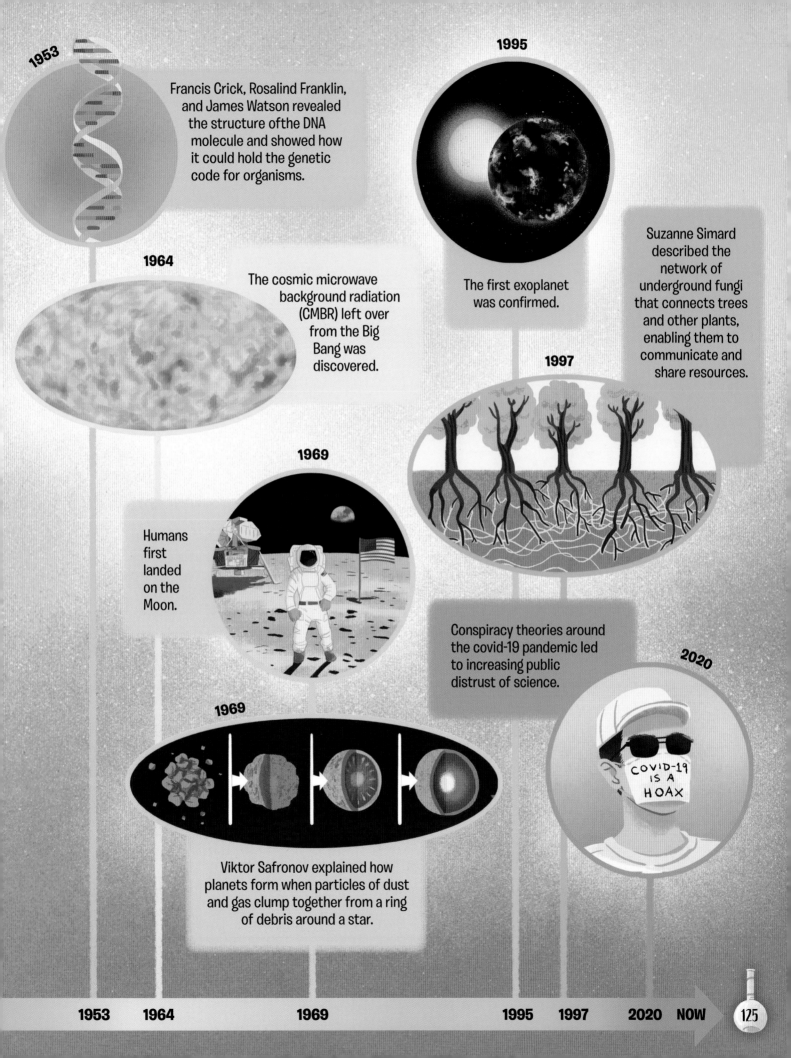

1953

Francis Crick, Rosalind Franklin, and James Watson revealed the structure of the DNA molecule and showed how it could hold the genetic code for organisms.

1995

The first exoplanet was confirmed.

Suzanne Simard described the network of underground fungi that connects trees and other plants, enabling them to communicate and share resources.

1964

The cosmic microwave background radiation (CMBR) left over from the Big Bang was discovered.

1997

1969

Humans first landed on the Moon.

Conspiracy theories around the covid-19 pandemic led to increasing public distrust of science.

2020

1969

Viktor Safronov explained how planets form when particles of dust and gas clump together from a ring of debris around a star.

COVID-19 IS A HOAX

1953   1964   1969   1995   1997   2020   NOW

125

GLOSSARY

anatomy The study of living bodies and how they work.

asteroid A large rocky body in space.

astronomical Relating to astronomy, the study of space.

atmosphere The layer of gases that surrounds a planet.

atom The smallest possible particle of a chemical element.

axis An imaginary line around which something rotates or is symmetrical.

botanist A scientist who studies plants.

buoyancy Being held up by water.

cell Tiny component of all living things. Cells are both structural and functional units.

circumference The distance around the edge of a circle.

cleavage plane The line along which a rock or mineral naturally breaks.

constellation Pattern or picture people see in the stars.

Coptic Of or relating to the Copts of ancient Egypt.

decipher Work out the meaning of.

dementia Loss of mental ability as a result of age or disease.

dislocated Moved out of place.

DNA Deoxyribonucleic acid, the chemical that makes up chromosomes and carries genetic information.

domesticated Made tame and changed in other ways to suit human purposes.

drag Slowing or resisting movement through a liquid or gas, by friction between an object and the particles of the liquid or gas.

eclipse One heavenly body passing in front of another and blocking some of its light. A solar eclipse happens when the Moon passes between Earth and the Sun.

electromagnetic spectrum The range of types of energy that travel through space in the form of waves, from radio waves to gamma rays.

element A fundamental chemical substance that can't be broken down into other substances. All matter is made of 118 chemical elements.

elliptical In the shape of an ellipse (oval).

enzyme A chemical in an organism that prompts or speeds up a chemical reaction, but isn't used up in the reaction.

epilepsy A medical condition that causes a person to have seizures.

equator An imaginary line around the middle of Earth, halfway between the North and South Poles.

experiment A rigorous test to try out a scientific idea.

fertilized Made able to grow into a new organism by bringing male and female cells together.

fluorescent Capable of absorbing light of a short wavelength and putting out light of a longer wavelength.

friction A force that acts to slow two objects moving against each other, or one moving over or through another.

genetics The study of heredity, of organisms passing on characteristics to their offspring or inheriting them from their parents.

geocentric With Earth in the middle.

geometry The branch of mathematics that deals with shapes, lines, points and spaces.

geothermal Using heat from deep inside Earth.

glaze Shiny glass-based layer, added to finish pottery.

habitat The place and environment in which an organism lives.

harpoon Pointed weapon used to hunt sea animals.

heliocentric With the Sun in the middle.

humors The four body fluids that ancient Greek medical theory supposed controlled health and sickness.

intangible Not touchable.

irrigation Providing water to crops.

lunar Relating to the Moon.

metamorphosis The process of changing body plan and shape that some animals undergo as they grow (for example, from tadpoles to frogs).

meteor Rock from space falling through Earth's atmosphere.

meteorologist A scientist who studies the weather.

microorganism Organism so small it can be seen only with a microscope.

migrate Move from one place to another.

mineralogy The study of rocks and minerals.

molecule Smallest component of a chemical substance which is only that substance.

mRNA vaccine A vaccine that prompts the body to respond to a protein on the surface of a virus, but doesn't use any of the actual virus.

mummify Preserve a dead body.

navigation Finding a way between two places.

nugget Small lump of metal.

ochre Clay containing iron oxide used as a pigment.

optics The study of light, lenses, and vision.

ore Rock that contains metal.

organism A living thing, such as a plant, animal, or fungus.

parasitic Living on another organism.

photosynthesis The process by which plants make sugar from water and gases.

plastic surgery Operations to change the appearance and structure of the body.

pollinate Move pollen from one flower to another, fertilizing a flower.

prehistoric From before the time people made written records, around 5,500 years ago.

quantitative Method of experimentation or observation that looks at measurable quantities and amounts.

radar Use of radio waves to bounce off objects and detect the "echo" to locate them.

reproduce Make more of (by breeding in animals and plants, or by dividing in cells).

satellite An object which orbits around a planet, star, or moon in space.

scientific method The way scientific experiments are carried out. A scientist sets up a hypothesis and tests it methodically to decide if their idea is correct or not.

smelt Heat ore to separate molten metal from the rock that contains it.

solar Relating to the Sun.

Sumerian Belonging to the ancient culture in Sumer, now Iraq.

suture A surgical stitch to hold a wound closed.

torsion Twisting through force.

vacuum Space containing nothing.

zoologist A scientist who studies animals.

INDEX